Intentional Dating

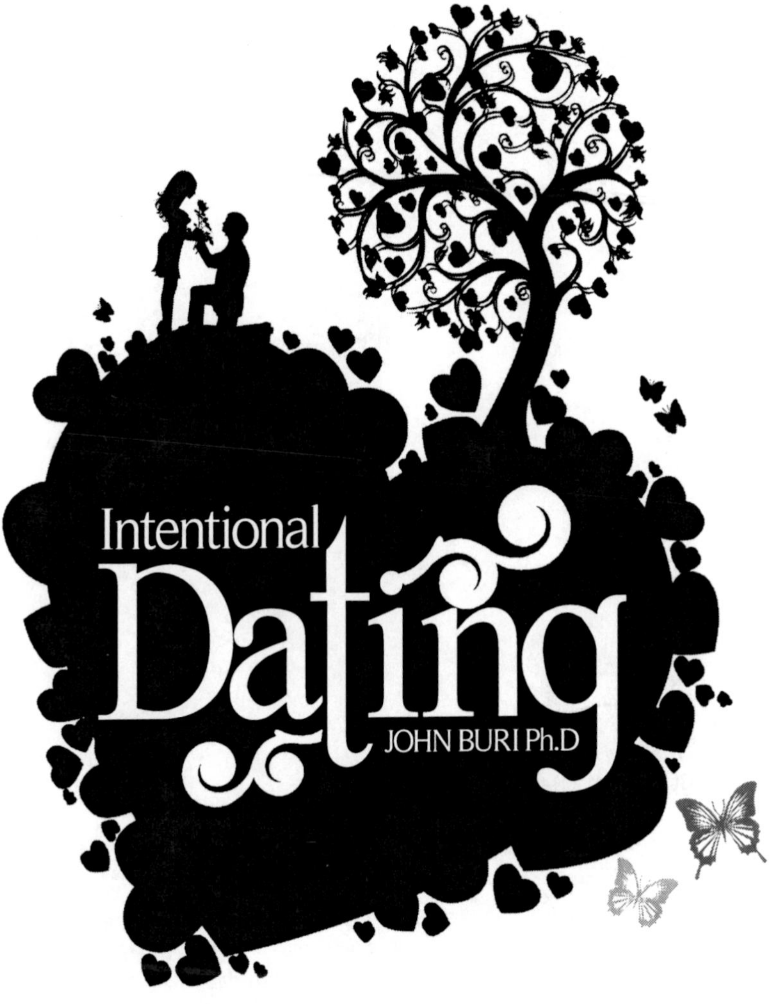

Intentional Dating

JOHN BURI Ph.D

When You're Ready To Leave Behind the Liars, Losers, and Lemons – 15 Keys To Finding Love for a Lifetime

ISBN: 978-1-948282-15-4
Intentional Dating

Yorkshire Publishing
3207 South Norwood Avenue
Tulsa, Oklahoma 74135
www.YorkshirePublishing.com
918.394.2665

To my wife—you are the love of a lifetime.

To my children—you had the wisdom to search for wonderful, loving, and life-giving spouses.

To our growing family—you are a joy day after day.

You all enrich my life beyond measure.
Thank you. I love you.

And to God—the fount of life and love.
Years ago you broke through in my life
and that changed everything.
Thank you. I am eternally grateful.

Contents

Introduction.......... 9
This Thing Called Love.......... 13
The Romantic Love Complex.......... 25
Eyes Wide Open.......... 39
What Is Dating for, Anyway?.......... 59
We Give Power to Those We Love.......... 73
Narcissism's First Cousin.......... 85
The Best Version of You.......... 97
Friendship: The Foundation of Marriage.......... 113
Marshmallows and Marriage.......... 129
Why Marshmallows Continue to Matter.......... 147
"How Do I Love Thee? Let Me Count the Ways..".......... 159
Gratitude.......... 171
The Love Bank.......... 187
Notes.......... 191
References.......... 217

Introduction

The Adventure of a Lifetime

Over the years, I have had the opportunity to be with several individuals as they have neared the end of their lives. Personally, this has been a very moving experience. It has also often proven to be quite enlightening. To spend time with people during this unique period in their lives—when they are inclined to look back and to reflect—can open a window into those things in life that are most important to us.

I can tell you that over all those years with all these people, I have yet to hear anyone say that they wish they had invested more time and effort in their careers. I have yet to have anyone tell me that they wish they had lived in bigger homes, or owned nicer cars, or had the money for more extravagant vacations. No, these things just haven't come up. But what I have heard over and over again is this: "I wish I had a more loving marriage." "I wish I had given more of my time and energy to my wife and my children." "I wish I had accumulated less stuff in my life, and instead, had amassed more love in my marriage."

Imagine that you were asked: "Given one wish, what would you most wish for?" Would it be for wealth? Power? A long life? A great job? When people have been asked this question, the vast majority of them have mentioned none of these. Instead, they have expressed a desire to love and to be loved—and not just for a week or a month or a year, but for a lifetime.[1]

That is the reason for this book. We are surrounded by news of failed marriages, unhappy spouses, and unfaithful partners. It's enough to discourage people from ever making their way down the aisle. Either that or you start to think that having a successful marriage is like buying a lottery ticket, and you simply hope that you are one of the lucky ones.

Would it help if I told you that the odds of having a stable and satisfying marriage are actually quite high—if you know what to look for? Would it help if I told you that most of what afflicts marriages can be remedied—if you know what to change? Would it help if I told you that we know what it takes to have a successful marriage—if you're willing to do it? This is all true, and this is what *Intentional Dating* is all about.

Imagine that there's an adventure just waiting for you. This is an adventure that is filled with all sorts of perks. All you need to do is find an able traveling companion, and you can embark on the adventure of a lifetime. Also, imagine that you are told that the journey will not always be easy, and that there will be pitfalls and some bumps on the road along the way, but that the adventure is worth it. Would you take that adventure? I would (and I have). That adventure is called marriage.

But for any challenging adventure, you want to prepare. As Oprah is accustomed to say, "When you know better, you do better." This book is about that preparation. Unfortunately, way too many people wait until they've said "I do" before they begin to look seriously at what it takes to be happily married. That would be like heading off to climb Mount Everest, and only after beginning the ascent giving thought to ropes, harnesses, pitons, quickdraws, carabiners, and crampons. The best time to prepare is before you ever begin the journey.

Is this adventure worth it? Unequivocally, yes. Did you know that married couples live longer and healthier lives, experience more frequent and more satisfying sex, are better off financially, and have greater overall life satisfaction?[2] But even more importantly, when marriage is done well, it is an ongoing source of love, life, and spirit-filled enthusiasm for living. This book is about doing it well.

My wife, Kathy, and I have been on this adventure together for over forty years. She is my best friend, and she is the best thing that has ever happened to me. She has helped to make this journey (called life) an amazing adventure.

As with virtually every couple, our experience has not always been easy; in fact, it has often resembled the scaling of a mountain. There have been rocky paths as well as easy foot trails. There have been steep inclines as well as simple passages. There have been times when I have taken the lead and provided direction and security, and there have been times when our roles have been reversed. There have even been times when the route has seemed impassable. Through it all, we have learned to be a team (a *we*), traveling side by side, enjoying the challenges—and the splendor—of this adventure together. My hope is that you too will find someone who has the qualities necessary to help make the journey of life one that is fulfilling, enriching, inspiring, and life-giving. That is the reason for this book.

This Thing Called Love

Love and Marriage

> I repeat the marriage vows that say: "I take my spouse for better or for worse, for richer or for poorer, in sickness or in health." When I make those vows, I probably hear the parts that say "better," "richer," and "health;" what about the parts saying "worse," "poorer," and "sickness?"
>
> Paul L. Bremer

Marriage is difficult.

This sort of statement seldom seems to surprise anyone. Married couples are well aware of it. Marriage therapists are in almost universal agreement about it. Even unmarried men and women know it; a very high percentage (86 percent) of young adults believe that marriage is hard work.[3] As counselor and author Michele Weiner put it, "The truth is, marriage is extremely hard work. Long-term marriage is not for sissies."[4]

And yet, when we look at the way we do love in this culture, there is a glaring disconnect. It is obvious that we marry for love; to suggest otherwise would border on the ridiculous. But the type of love we regularly practice prior to marriage provides very poor preparation for marriage itself.

The problem is that what many of us are searching for in the name of love is not love at all. Rather, what has most captured our attention is the elusive, but ever-enticing, in-love experience.[5]

Love? Or an In-Love Experience?

> Intensity of attraction is a beautiful thing. But to label it love is both foolish and dangerous. What love requires on top of instant emotion is time, shared experiences and feelings, and a long and tempered bond between two people.
>
> Stanton Peele

Take, for example, the effortlessness of the in-love experience. It is almost always easy; that's why we call it "falling" in love. How much effort does it take to fall? But the suggestion that love is effortless is ridiculous. It ranks as one of the more stupid assertions ever made about love; in fact, it probably ranks right up there with the line from the 1970s movie *Love Story*: "Love means never having to say you're sorry."

Or consider the fact that the in-love experience typically serves to assuage the painfulness of life. But love often does not. In fact, what many of us have discovered (the hard way, by actually loving) is that when we truly do love, sometimes the struggles of life increase rather than decrease. After all, we are no longer simply consumed by our own world of concerns, but now there is someone else whose concerns we also care about, and (hopefully) help to carry. No, if your desire is to find relief from the painfulness of life, then I would recommend that you distance yourself from love.[6]

The same is true of life's responsibilities. How many people searching for love are longing for greater responsibility? To suggest such a thing would offend the modern sensibilities of many men and women. But the truth is this: love does not lessen our responsibilities. In-loveness may, but love does not. On the contrary, love by its very nature carries with it more responsibilities.

And then there is the issue of being accountable to, and for, another. Merely being in love has virtually no accountability attached to it. As long as two people experience in-loveness, then they stay together. But once that experience of being in love begins to wane, then the couple is free to go their separate ways. This does not bare the remotest resemblance to love. With love, there is accountability to (and oftentimes for) another.

No, love is difficult. And that is why marriage is difficult. There are hundreds of couples who end up in marriage therapists' offices every day. For many of them, it has been a mistaken notion of love that has led them to this difficult and painful place in their marriage.

Does it strike anyone else as odd? We spend years of our lives dating, pursuing this thing we call love, only to find out that much of what we have been doing is only marginally related to the end goal of marriage. And then we wonder why the failure rate for marriage is so high.

The Myth of Romantic Love

> The Prince rushed up and lifted her out of the casket. He told her all that had happened and begged her to be his bride. Snow White consented with sparkling eyes, so they rode away to the Prince's home where they prepared for a gay and gala wedding...and they all lived happily ever after.
>
> Snow White and the Seven Dwarfs
> (Wanda Gag, translator)

There are probably no notions about love that have done more damage (to individuals, to couples, and to society) than the beliefs surrounding romantic love. It starts when we are very young—with the fairy tales, which nearly always end with "and they lived happily ever after." Unfortunately, none of these fairy tales tell us how many frogs we need to kiss before we'll find our prince. Nor do they tell us the truth. Princes don't exist. (By the way, neither do princesses.) These fairy tales have us believing (from a very young age) that when we find "the one," then happily-ever-after will be ours.

This myth of romantic love is then perpetuated by the media—music, movies, magazines, books. The terminology varies, but the message is the same, and we are bombarded daily by this myth of romantic love: "You can't help but fall in love when you meet the right person." "If you're really meant for each other, then your relationship won't be work." "When you find 'the one,' you'll know; and if you don't know, then this can't be 'the one.'" "Love is easy when you're with the person you're meant to be with."

Let's face it: romantic love sells. It sells music, it sells movies, it sells magazines, and it sells books. And admittedly, there is something about this view of love that is very appealing. After all, the implication is that if you can find the right person, then loving won't be so much work. In fact, if you're with the right person, than all of life will be easier. There is something very alluring about this message.

And quite honestly, this cultural emphasis on in-loveness would not be so damaging if it had not so easily seeped into the mind-set of serious, God-loving women and men. The language is a little different, but the message is the same. If you fall in love with the person meant for you, then love (and life) will all go well for you; but now, the person meant for you has been ordained by God: "God has someone out there for you. You just have to find that person." "Marriages are made in heaven. Don't settle for someone who is not your soul mate." "God has had someone for you from the beginning of time, and when you meet them, you'll know."

I realize that most of us are looking for authentic love and that many of us are seeking a happy, loving, and life-giving marriage. But one thing is clear: a romantic view of love will not get us either of these. The evidence is clear; in-loveness is a very poor predictor of both authentic love and successful marriages.[7]

Eric and Allie

> "And they lived happily ever after" is one of the most tragic sentences in literature. It's tragic because it's a falsehood. It is a myth that has led generations to expect something from marriage that is not possible.
>
> Joshua Liebman

Eric and Allie were a young couple who came to see me during their second year of marriage. They had met six years earlier when they were students at the same university, and soon after they met, they were sure they were meant to be together. Eric was twenty-eight, good-looking and articulate, with a lively sense of humor. Allie, twenty-seven, was an attractive and engaging young woman, the type of person who lights up a room as soon as she walks in. Each was successful in their careers—Eric as a financial advisor and Allie as a teacher. I remember being struck early on by the impression that this was an attractive, bright, and caring couple. My time with them only served to reinforce this initial impression.

As I first began to meet with Eric and Allie, I was puzzled by their presenting problems. They seemed to be a couple experiencing the typical ebb and flow of married life. They enjoyed spending time together, whether it was going to a movie, grabbing dinner, or simply hanging out at home. But they also experienced areas of disagreement in their life together: Do you put the dirty dishes in the dish washer, or do you simply leave them in the sink to be dealt with later? Do you leave your shoes and coat by the front door when you come home, or do you put them away in the closet? Do you call to let your spouse know when you're going to be late, or do you assume that they'll figure it out?

Needless to say, Eric and Allie had some work to do in order to get on the same page in their relationship. The problem was that they hadn't expected marriage to be work. You see, they had each absorbed many of the beliefs emanating from the myth of romantic love. They really had bought into the idea that true love is not work—at least it's not work if what you have going for you really is true love. The problem is: this is a lie. It's simply not true, and anytime we hold on to something that isn't true, in the end, that lie will lead to our undoing.

Believing Something That Is Not True

> We have a picture of the perfect partner, but we marry an imperfect person. Then we have two options. Tear up the picture, and accept the person, or tear up the person and accept the picture.
>
> J. Grant Howard Jr.

Think about it. If I believe that true love is going to have few difficulties and struggles, but then I begin to experience the normal speed bumps along the road of married life, then what else am I to conclude except that what we have must not be true love? If I am convinced that true love means continually experiencing in-loveness with my wife, but I wake up some morning with the residue of last night's disagreement still lingering in our bed, then I have one of two choices—either I can realize that my thinking about love is all messed up or else I can decide that what my wife and I have isn't really love after all.

Eric and Allie found—as is true of all couples who say "I do"—that married life requires work. To their dismay, they discovered that love doesn't just happen simply because they were now together day after day. To their disbelief, they began to encounter the reality that happiness is not an effortless byproduct of two people who have experienced being in love.[8]

And in those moments when they naturally and inevitably no longer experienced the in-loveness that had propelled them toward marriage, they each began to experience doubts: "How could this be 'the one' when it is so much work?" "If what we really have is love, then why am I not as happy/satisfied as I thought I was going to be?" "Isn't love supposed to just happen? But it isn't just happening for us. What's wrong with our marriage?" "How could this really be love when there are so many times that I'm not feeling in love?"

I wish I could tell you that Eric and Allie made it, that they are still married, living their lives somewhere in happily-ever-after land. But unfortunately, I can't. Eric and Allie's marriage was sabotaged by the myth of romantic love. In the end, the doubts won, and Eric and Allie lost. Disillusioned, disappointed, and discouraged, rather than give up their false notions of love, Eric and Allie decided to give up on each other.

Sometimes I still think about Eric and Allie, and when I do, I always end up saddened. They are such good people and they had so much going for them, but they insisted on believing something that isn't true.

Not a Love Cynic

> If the higher companionship which love should be does not make men and women nobler, more generous, more ready to sacrifice, then there is a suspicion that their love is not love but a combination of egoisms.
>
> Ernest Dimnet

Don't get me wrong here. I'm not a love cynic. In fact, over the years my children have repeatedly accused me of being a "hopeless romantic." There were the flowers (with the sappy love notes attached) that frequently appeared on the dining room table for their mother. This was something that my children had little appreciation for; after all, the flowers kept dying. My children also observed (with at least a modicum of indifference) the frequent romantic evenings that my wife and I enjoyed, although they had to observe them from a distance—from home. And then there were the weekends away (just for two) and the little candies left on the pillow (placed there after all our children were in bed) and the stick-em love notes left on the bathroom mirror. I am actually quite romantic.

You see, I know that if a marriage is to thrive, it needs lots of romance.[9] And not just when somebody is interested in making love. I am actually saddened by the number of couples I have known for whom romance has only become a way to get sex. I have heard from women more times than I care to count sentiments like the following: "I don't want him to be romantic. The only time he's ever romantic is when he's interested in sex. I would like him to be romantic simply because he loves me and he wants to let me know, not so that there will be some payoff for him."

The truth is—most of us know how to be romantic. We've been romantic many times in the past, and we will no doubt be romantic many times in the future. The problem is not that we don't know how. The problem is in the why. Too often we use romance to get, rather than to give.

For example, some people will use romance to get sex. Others will use romance to manipulate people to their wishes; it is sometimes amazing what people will agree to in the midst of a romantic moment. Still others will use romance to hide their true intent; romance can be quite deceptive. And still others will use romance as an escape from the harshness of living. In each case, romance is used for the purposes of receiving, not for the purposes of giving. And when we use romance for what we are getting out of it, then it can hardly be called love.

Romance is not meant to be expressed because of what we are going to get. Romance is intended for the other. It is something to be given, not something to be used. It is an expression of affection for the other, a token of love, a way of letting the other person know that they are appreciated and valued. Whenever an expression of romance is more about receiving than giving, then one should reasonably wonder how much loving is actually taking place in the exchange.

I sometimes think of romance as love's Vitamin D. A deficiency in Vitamin D has been linked to loss of energy, chronic pain, depression, increased vulnerability to cancer, reduced life expectancy, and cardiovascular problems. A deficiency in romance will have the same effects on your relationship. What was said of Vitamin D by natural health researcher Mike Adams[10] can also be said of romance: "It is safe, effective, and available free of charge. If it could be patented, it would be hyped as the greatest breakthrough in history. It's that good."

So it is not romance that is in question here. Not at all. If you want a healthy love between you and your beloved, then be romantic—and not just when you're looking to get something. The problem is that many people hold the mistaken notion that somehow romantic love (the in-love experience) constitutes the essence of love. Anytime we buy into the false notion that when it comes to love, the heart of the matter is simply a matter of the heart, then we are destined for an authentic love failure.

Some of the Consequences

> When true love comes, that which is counterfeit will be recognized. For someday, it will rain on the picnic, ants will sting, mosquitoes will bite, and you will get indigestion from the potato salad. There will be no stars in your eyes, no sunsets on your horizon. Love will be in black and

> white with no piped-in music. But you will say "forever" because love is a choice you have made.
>
> Ruth Senter

A long-time friend, Matt, called one day to see if we could get together. Matt is a bright IT guy, a little bit on the introverted side but quite amiable and outgoing once he gets to know you. He had recently pursued a new job opportunity in which he had to travel quite a bit, so it wasn't until two weeks later that we were able to meet for a beer and some apps at a restaurant near campus.

It didn't take Matt long to bring up why he wanted to get together. He had met someone. During a recent business trip to Houston, he had connected with a waitress, and he was convinced that this was the person he was meant to be with.

Matt explained it this way. "You know, John, when Meghan and I married six years ago we were madly in love with each other. I felt like I had arrived. I was so happy whenever we were together, and the love between us just happened. It was effortless. Just the way it's supposed to be. But slowly over the past couple of years, our marriage has started to get a little stale. I might be wrong, but I just don't think that this is the way it's supposed to be. You know, when you love someone, then that love should just happen. It shouldn't be work. And it definitely shouldn't go stale like an old loaf of bread.

"Well, I met this woman in Houston, and we clicked right away. The chemistry was amazing. You know how when you meet the right person, you can't help but fall in love. Well, that was us. I think I've finally found the person I was meant to be with all along."

Despite my encouragement to the contrary, Matt ended up leaving Meghan, and he moved to Houston to pursue this new love of his life. I wish I could tell you that this was the one Matt was meant to be with and that they are still basking effortlessly in their love for one another, but unfortunately, I can't. This new in-loveness experience in Houston lasted less than a year before it too went stale.

The problem is this. Sooner or later, for every couple, romantic love wanes. It is a natural consequence of any in-love experience. Unfortunately, way too many couples decide in the face of this reality to jettison the relationship just when the opportunity for true love has presented itself. Matt was faced with a choice. He could continue to pursue the in-love experience that had captured his adolescent heart years earlier. Or he could grab hold of the more genuine and adult notion of love, and go home and embrace the effort, struggles, responsibilities, and accountability that true love necessitates. Unfortunately, Matt decided to hold on to an adolescent fantasy.

Key No. 1

Looking for that elusive in-love experience is arguably our greatest pitfall to actually finding the healthy love we desire.

By its very nature, in-loveness is fleeting and unstable, and therefore anything that is built on it will be fleeting and unstable.

If you want love, don't be deceived by in-loveness. Instead, look for those qualities that can help form a foundation for lifelong love.

The Romantic Love Complex

Our Obsession with Romantic Love

> Falling in love is easy. Growing in love must be worked at with determination.
>
> Lesley Barefoot

Several years ago, sociologist William Goode stated that all cultures, both historical and contemporary, vary along a continuum of romantic love.[11] At one end of the continuum, Goode argued, are those cultures in which romantic love is typically viewed as absurd, and for the most part, unhealthy. For example, the Greek philosopher Plato suggested that romantic love is comparable to "a grave mental illness." In such cultures, romantic love is considered laughable (at best) and tragically destructive (at worst).

Near the middle of this continuum are those cultures in which romantic love is not so clearly and so overtly held in disdain. In such cultures, there are no prohibitive admonitions against romantic love, and in fact, couples may even be encouraged to experience this type of love with their spouse. But even in such cases, romantic love would not be viewed as substantive. Simply put, romantic love might be a nice add-on, but it is largely seen as irrelevant. It is simply not something to which a person would give credence when it comes to making significant life decisions.

At the opposite end of the continuum is what Goode called the "Romantic Love Complex." Cultures at this end of the spectrum give considerable prominence to romantic love. They tend to view falling in love as both reasonable and beneficial, and they see romantic love as an important, if not *the most important*, component in any significant dating and/or marriage relationship. In other words, in such cultures, romantic love has been normalized; it has come to be viewed as the most natural (and in some ways, most desirable) thing in the world.

Where do we in modern Western culture fit along this continuum of romantic love? There are four primary components of the Romantic Love Complex: (1) Love at First Sight, (2) Love Is Blind, (3) Love Conquers All, and (4) Love Is Passionate.[12] Where do we fall on each of these? No news flash here. We celebrate them in popular song, we provide detailed accounts of them in movie after movie, and we chronicle the ups and downs of them in a parade of celebrity magazines. All of this has left its mark. Without a doubt, it can be said that we are at the extreme end of the Romantic Love Complex.

No. 1: Love at First Sight

> The person who only or chiefly chooses for beauty, will in time, find the same reason for another choice.
>
> Mary Astell

Approximately 60 percent of Americans believe in love at first sight. Furthermore, over 50 percent say they have experienced it.[13] In light of the weighty decisions many of us make in the name of love, these are some staggering figures.

Think about it—what can we actually know about a person based on first sight? Essentially, their physical appearance, and that's about it. I'm sorry to have to be the one to dispel any illusions, but physical attractiveness is not a good predictor of love—at least, not if what we mean by love is anything beyond an in-love experience.

Sure, physical attractiveness is, well, attractive—sugar candy for the eye—but what does it tell us about the person behind the candy? Typically not much. Isn't it odd that even with dating services that offer quite a bit of information about prospective partners, users will nearly always start with the pictures and then pursue further information only for those individuals who have met certain attractiveness criteria. And this is true even when the pictures are presented *after* the information.[14]

Many of us claim to know that beauty is only skin deep, and that it tells us very little about whether a particular individual will be a good lover (beyond the transitory experience of in-loveness), and yet we continue to make initial love selections based on it. Is this puzzling to anyone besides me? The truth is: virtually all of us (if we live long enough) are going to resemble a minivan more than a sports car. And yet, time after time we pass over the slightly paunchy prospective in favor of the eye candy, even though such things are meaningless when it comes to being a good spouse or a good parent.

Physical appearance just doesn't tell us a whole lot about who will put effort into a relationship, or who will be willing to endure your pain along with you, or who will be accountable and responsible in love. The bottom line is this: as long as people continue to pursue something as transitory as physical attractiveness, then what they're going to get from love is little more than a transitory experience. As an old Chinese adage suggests: "If you continue to do what you have always done, you will continue to get what you have always gotten."

No. 2: Love Is Blind

> True love has clarity and honesty. It can see through the fog. When people are blinded by love, then they are either infatuated or obsessed, but they are not in love.
>
> Bridget Webber

It's not unusual to find that when people are in love, they can be fairly oblivious to certain things that should not be overlooked. For example, Melanie had only been dating Shane for three months when he was picked up for his fourth DUI. When I asked her if she was at all concerned about Shane's behavior, Melanie commented, "Not really. It doesn't seem like a problem to me. Besides, all he really needs is the love of a good woman, and now he's got that." Melanie didn't seem to be at all aware of the fact that the love of a good woman to which she was referring had not in any way prevented Shane from getting his most recent DUI.

Then there's Jacob. Jacob was a twenty-four-year old construction worker who fell in love with a recent divorcee, Kristin. It didn't take long before Jacob and Kristin decided to marry. It was only after they did that Jacob began to notice Kristin's relationship with her mother. On occasion, Kristin would yell and scream at her mother, sometimes letting loose a long stream of expletives. As Jacob thought about it, he vaguely remembered that this had happened before, but he was surprised to realize that he had not really paid much attention to it—until now. As you may have guessed, the reason I am aware of Jacob's story is because he came to see me about his volatile marriage. As is true of all problem behaviors, being unaware of them does not make them any less problematic—and eventually they will come home to roost. It was only a matter of time before Jacob ended up on the receiving end of Kristin's angry tirades.

While in the grip of love, we can so easily be blind to negative behaviors, often even interpreting them as positives. The control freak will be viewed as a take-charge type of guy, laziness will be seen as laid-back and relaxed, and the financial tightwad will be perceived as thrifty and a good money manager. Over and over again, the love blinders go to work, misleading those in love to interpret the immature as childlike, the reckless as adventuresome, the overbearing as firm, the irresponsible as spontaneous, the unfeeling as strong, the smothering as caring, the workaholic as ambitious, the compulsive as neat, and the narcissist as self-confident.

I have to admit. In some ways, I can understand this. When we are in the throes of in-loveness, we are essentially in a drug-induced state. Biochemicals in the brain (for example: dopamine, norepinephrine, and phenylethylamine) begin to whirl around in a love potion so strong that black will sometimes appear white and white will sometimes appear black. So in some ways, I get it. A certain amount of blindness can be expected when people fall in love. It's simply a drug-induced state.[15]

But what I don't get is this: why would we encourage this love-blindness as normal? Rather than warn people against this chemically-induced state—so they can make some necessary adjustments in their love perceptions—why do we insist on encouraging it as an expected part of being in love?[16] In what other area of living would we ever want to suggest that blinded is better than sighted, inattentive better than mindful, unaware better than observant, and ignorant better than astute? But somehow, when it comes to love, we are encouraged to accept the aberrant as normal. In fact, this is so widespread and so entrenched that if a friend were to bravely ask us about our partner's angry outbursts and his belittling remarks, we can easily end up going off in a huff, offended that someone who calls themselves a friend would ever suggest such a thing. Sometimes these blinders are all but superglued in place.

No. 3: Love Conquers All

The sparkle of a new relationship is always temporary.

Linda and Charlie Bloom

I love the ocean. I love walking into it. I love playing in it. I love letting it toss me around. I love simply looking at it. One day when I was sitting on the shore watching it, I was suddenly startled by the realization that the waves of the ocean never stop. As far out as you can see, the waves continue to roll in. Some of these waves amount to just a little surge of water. They bump up against your legs, splash in your face, and then (for the most part) head harmlessly back out to sea. But other waves come at you with a vengeance. They give you a water-wedgie, knock you off you feet, and then face-plant you in the shore. In the wake of these waves, you find yourself picking sand out of your shorts for a week.

In many ways, life is like this. The "waves of life" never stop. They just keep rolling in. Some of these waves bump up against us. They get our attention, they're a hassle, and we have to deal with them, but they aren't terribly disruptive to life. But others of these waves pack quite a wallop. They knock us right off our psychological feet. They can leave us picking emotional sand from our souls for weeks (if not years).

Now I don't know about you, but I've known a lot of people who have wanted love to somehow quell the crashing waves of life. In their heart of hearts, they have believed that if they can somehow find their one true love, then all of life's problems will be tamed, and all of life's struggles and heartaches will be conquered.

But let me tell you—it isn't going to happen. Simply put, there is no such love. The waves of life are not going to cease. And on top of that, the ones we love sometimes (often?) become a source of those waves.

In a sample of over one thousand college students, 82 percent agreed that there are no difficulties or differences that can come between a couple if they are in love with each other enough.[17] I would be a rich man right now if I had a dollar for every couple who marched forward—he an earnest vegetarian, she an avid meat-eater; he an avowed agnostic, she a devout Christian; he a happy-go-lucky freeloader, she a staunch workaholic; he a conscientious saver, she a carefree spender—convinced that love conquers all, only to find the differences between them dashing their love against the rocks of reality. And as many of us know, it doesn't take differences as stark as these to generate waves large enough to swamp a relationship.

In-loveness will not save us from the waves of life. In fact, nothing short of death will save us from these waves. Coming to grips with this reality is essential to growing up. People who embrace this truth—and at the same time know that life is good, that it's worth living, and that they can still be happy (even though the waves of life are not ever going to stop)—these people have taken a huge step toward adulthood.

As you think about love—not in-loveness, but love—imagine facing these waves with someone who understands that authentic love requires effort, someone who is willing to responsibly wrestle alongside you against all that life may toss your way, someone who will be accountable to you (and for you) as you face the waves of life together. That is the kind of love most of us long for, and that is the kind of love this book is about.

No. 4: Love Is Passionate

If passion drives you, let reason hold the reins.

Benjamin Franklin

Among the four characteristics of the Romantic Love Complex, I doubt that any of them is more alive and well today than the belief that love is passionate. For example, it is commonly acknowledged in our culture that if you love someone, then you will feel passion for that individual; and if there isn't passion, then this is an obvious indication that you are not in love. To many of us, this just seems like common sense.

Therefore, we have come to accept as perfectly logical the idea that if a couple experiences the rush associated with passion, then they are in love. And if (when) they no longer experience this rush with each other, then they are no longer in love. We have so strongly come to accept this as truth that when college students were asked if they would pursue a divorce if the passion disappeared from their marriage, over 50 percent said yes.[18]

Once again, please don't get me wrong here. I am not a passion cynic. I am not trying to suggest that passion is irrelevant to love. Just the opposite. Passion is a very important component of love. But passion alone does not love make.

In fact, those who are inclined to mistake passion for love are also those who tend to value passion more than they value their partner. For such individuals, the words "I love you" may at times be uttered, but what is really being said is typically something more like: "I love the passion we experience together." For such individuals, the experience of love is really more about them than it is about you. Anytime we pursue passion for passion's sake, the rush we get is more about us than it is about love. And let's face it: mistaking passion for love is not going to help us discern those who are likely to be good candidates for the stable, reliable, caring, long-term partner that any reasonable person would want as a spouse.

In reality, passion is valuable not for the rush it gives us (as enjoyable as that rush might be). But rather, passion is important because, as human beings, we are inclined to suffer for those things (and those people) for whom we have passion.

The first thing I ever cared about beyond my own self-interest—in other words, the first thing for which I ever had enough passion that I was willing to suffer for it—was basketball. In fact, to this day I have certain body parts (hips, back, a knee) that don't work very well because of that first passion. Would I do it differently if I had it to do all over again? Definitely not. Passion has a way of bringing life. It creates things that the passionless can only dream about.

So am I opposed to passion? No. In fact, a key to successful marriages is the ability to maintain passion in the relationship.[19] I don't know whether you've ever noticed it, but couples who have worked to sustain passion in their marriage have a certain pizzazz to them. They radiate life. Just being around them is invigorating. And if you watch such couples, you'll notice that they are attentive to each other, that they care about each other, and that they find ways to serve each other. In a word, they are willing to sacrifice for each other.

No, I am not opposed to passion. Those couples who experience passion are too clearly willing to suffer for each other and for the good of their relationship. Passion is too central to the sacrificial nature of authentic love to be regarded as inconsequential. But what I am opposed to is any suggestion that passion is the primary criterion that will tell us whether what two people are experiencing is love. This may be true of in-loveness, but it is not true of love.

A Dozen (and Counting)

> Unless we change directions, we're likely to end up where we're headed.
>
> Old Chinese Proverb

By her own admission, Alissa has been in more relationships than she could possibly keep track of. She claims that she quit counting at a dozen. It's not that Alissa has simply been going through guys like a series of restaurants, briefly sampling what's on the menu and then moving on to the next one.

Granted, some people do spend their dating years this way—the goal: sample as many delicacies as possible, but never settle on any one dish for too long. Needless to say, this has been known to register quite high on the pleasure meter, but seldom does it produce a suitable long-term marriage partner.[20]

But marriage is exactly what Alissa has been looking for. From the beginning, her desire has been to find a man who would be a good husband and father. As she described it, "I have been looking for someone that I can love for a lifetime and who will love me in return. A man to whom I can give myself and with whom I can share all that life has to offer. A person with whom I can have children, and together we can raise a family and make a home."

Why the struggle? Why over a dozen guys (and counting)?

Admittedly, part of the problem for Alissa (as well as for thousands of other women like her) can be found in the fact that fewer and fewer men seem interested in the prospects of marriage. After all, as many men will tell you, just because you like what's on the menu doesn't mean you have to go and buy the whole restaurant. But as is true for many other women as well, Alissa found that the blame for her non-marital woes could not be placed solely on the shoulders of all those commitment-phobic men.

Are You In Love with Him?

> Insanity is doing the same thing over and over again and expecting different results.
>
> Bill O'Hanlon

In 1967, young adults were asked this question: "If a man or woman had all the qualities you desired in a mate, would you marry this person if you were not in love with him or her?" At that time, 76 percent of the sampled women and 35 percent of the men said yes. Just twenty years later, these percentages went down to 20 percent for women and 14% percent for men. And more recently, in one of our studies completed this past year here in the Twin Cities, only 10 percent of those sampled stated that they would likely marry someone with whom they were not in love, even if that person possessed a whole host of desirable qualities.[21]

It is clear that we marry for love—or should I say—we marry for in-loveness. But the problem is this. We are as likely to experience in-loveness with someone who is blatantly ill-prepared for marriage as with someone who would be an excellent marriage partner. In fact, we are as likely to experience in-loveness with an absolute jerk (or jerkette) as we are with someone who is genuinely a good person.[22] Furthermore, there are many who would make a wonderful marriage partner, but who never make it out of the box—because that elusive in-loveness is missing.

When Alissa first came to talk with me, she admitted that she had already passed on many men who would likely have been good marriage material. There was Robert. "Robert and I started dating when we were nineteen," Alissa told me, "and we dated for almost a year. He was steady and kind-hearted. Always good-natured. And I knew that I could count on him. If he said that he was going to be somewhere or do something, I knew that he was going to be true to his word. I liked him, and he was enjoyable to be with, but you know, I just wasn't that into him. We just didn't have that spark, that connection. I can't quite put my finger on it, but he just didn't feel like the one."

Alissa went on to describe another dozen men, all of whom sounded from her description like very viable candidates for marriage. But in each case, she "just wasn't feeling it." And so she continued on her heroic search for our cultural version of the holy grail. Alissa (like so many other women—and men) had become convinced that marriage should happen only after two people have experienced that "spark" or that "something" which would make it clear that a lifelong commitment is viable. And even though Alissa admitted that it wasn't always clear just what that "spark" would feel like, she was nonetheless certain that she would know it once she experienced it.

Unfortunately (for Alissa, as well as for the millions of other women—and men—who are looking for it), such a level of in-loveness doesn't exist. It's a fairy tale, a fantasy. It's an elusive dream, one from which healthy love requires that we wake up.

The way we are doing this thing called love needs a reality check. There are thousands of women out there, none of whom may turn your crank every time you look at her, but all of whom would be loving, energetic wives and great mothers. There are thousands of men out there who may not be as charming, good looking, and exciting as Brad Pitt, but they are reliable and hardworking men, and they would love you, appreciate you, and be faithful to you, and they'd be fantastic dads.

We have to get to a place where we realize that in the end, how hot he was at the beginning just doesn't matter. When you look like death warmed over because of the flu, and he is left to change the newborn baby's diaper and clean up the three-year old's vomit, and he manages to squeeze in making dinner and taking out the garbage, it's doubtful that in-loveness is going to be on your mind. But love? How could you not love a guy like that?

Key No. 2

For anyone who hopes to have a good chance of finding stable, healthy, and supportive love, the romantic love blinders have to come off.

Simply put, romantic love is inherently deceptive. It can happen with almost anyone. It tells us virtually nothing about the person with whom it has happened. And as many of us can personally attest, we can fall in love with many individuals who are not steadfast and stable enough to sustain the sort of love that healthy, live-giving marriages require.

Authentic love results from the choices we make, not from an experience of falling. If we are ever going to realize authentic love, then we will need to choose wisely.

Eyes Wide Open

The First-Six-Months Test

> When you learn to see people with your head, and not just with your eyes, you will attract much better partners into your life.
>
> Barbara De Angelis

We each have patterns of behavior—for example, how we spend our time in a typical day, how we normally respond in various situations, how we regularly treat people, how we routinely handle stress, and how we ordinarily react when things don't go our way. Day in and day out, we each have habitual patterns of behavior, and it should not come as a surprise to anyone that these regular and routine behavior patterns can have devastating consequences for marital success. But what might surprise some people is that several of these highly destructive behavior patterns are actually out there in the open, in plain sight, long before the marriage bells ever begin to ring. In fact, some of these unpleasant behaviors are present within the first few months of dating. I call it the "First-Six-Months Test."

Often, people will reason that any behavior patterns that are so destructive that they have the power to undermine a marriage must be the sorts of things that can't really be detected until much later in the relationship. After all, how could something so harmful be so obvious, and yet not be noticed? But the truth is, some of these highly destructive behavior patterns are already clearly visible within the first six months (or so) of dating. It is as if there is a large neon sign flashing: "Warning! Unhealthy, destructive behaviors ahead. Proceed with caution." Unfortunately, despite their blatant presence, many men and women don't read the signs.

Do you ever find yourself—as an objective observer—spending time with a couple and then walking away wondering: "Why is she staying with him?" "Why is he putting up with all her crap?" "What does she see in him?" "Why can't they see how unhealthy they are for each other?"

These are the sorts of behaviors that are key to the First-Six-Months Test. They are those patterns of behavior that are out there in the open for all to see. And yet, even though they are as blatant as the elephant in the living room, way too many dating men and women fail to take note of them, often with nasty consequences.

How Does Your Partner Treat People?

> The fragrance of what you give away stays with you.
>
> Earl Allen

A student named Melanie blurted out in class one day, "How could I have been so stupid? It was my first date with this guy; his name is Joe. We were at a restaurant. I had ordered a cheeseburger with fries, and when I reached for the ketchup, the bottle was empty. Joe suddenly yelled at the waitress, 'Hey, can we get some ketchup over here!' At the time, I thought, 'Oh, he's going to watch out for me. He's going to be attentive to what I want.' I thought it was sort of endearing. Now I know better. How could I have been so stupid?"

Be awake. Be alert. Watch how the person you are dating treats others.[23] The "others" may be waitresses, drivers on the road, salespeople, janitors, friends, parking lot attendants, coworkers, siblings, roommates, parents, or teachers.

Keep your eyes wide open. One of the very best predictors of an unhappy marriage is negativity.[24] So is this person negative? Do they tend to be harsh with other people, whether to their face or in how they talk about them behind their back? Are they demanding? Are they rude or condescending? Do they sulk and mope? Are they trudging through life, dour and sullen, leaving a dreary trail for anyone in their wake? This person may treat you differently now, but that will not be the case later. As Melanie found out, it never is. It's just a matter of time before you end up being treated just like everyone else. In fact, if a relationship makes it all the way to marriage, you can put a person's current behavior under a microscope and that will give you a very good idea of what they will be like after you marry them.

I am frequently puzzled when I meet a dating couple and one of them oozes negativity. I keep wondering what their partner sees in them. Why isn't the partner aware of this person's disagreeableness? Why can't they see how gloomy and morose they are? And if they are aware of it, why do they continue to put up with it?

You see, when we tolerate an unhealthy behavior—for example, when we continue to give ourselves in love to someone who is rude, demanding, and inconsiderate, or to someone who is dreary, glum, and despondent—then we end up reinforcing that behavior. This is one of those rules in life that you can count on; those behaviors that are reinforced are going to be repeated. In other words, the negativity is going to happen again, and in all likelihood, it's going to increase in frequency and intensity. As long as we put up with such unhealthy behavior, it's going to grow; the individual is going to become even more negative than before.[25]

As Melanie found out, sometimes the First-Six-Months Test only takes a few hours—if we are willing to watch. Unfortunately, Melanie was not. She dated Joe for over a year before she became aware of how poorly he was treating lots of people in his life—eventually even her.

Get a Life

> The greatest waste in the world is often the difference between what we are and what we could be.
>
> Ben Herbster

Brooke had a long history of dating guys whose lives were in a perpetual holding pattern. There was David, who after barely graduating from high school, lived with his parents for the next seven years while doing a variety of odd jobs, just enough to give him the money he needed to support his active nightlife. Then there was Peter, who spent most of his time day after day playing online video games with people all over the world. Peter was followed by Patrick, a self-professed writer/musician who spent his days dreamily strumming on his guitar and his evenings exchanging lyrics in one coffee shop after another, convinced that one day he would be discovered. After Patrick, there was Joel, a bright young man who left college after one semester so that he could pursue his dream of getting rich quick through online poker; he is now the unmarried father of three and he bags groceries part-time in a local supermarket. Finally, there was Leon, who dropped out of high school when he was seventeen (because "Who needs this boring stuff anyway?"), pursued a life of virtual cyberhibernation, and is now, at the age of twenty-eight, trying to get a job (without any formal training) as a computer analyst.

In each case, Brooke was there for these men, helping to support them in their nonlife. Each of them expressed hopes and aspirations for where they wanted to be—David, an engineer; Peter, a creator of video games; Patrick, an American Idol star; Joel, a poker success; and Leon, a computer programmer. Unfortunately, none of these men showed any concrete steps toward achieving these aspirations. Simply put, they failed to walk the talk.[26]

Yet, Brooke was, in turn, in love with each of these men. And being in love, she was more than happy to do what she could to help them achieve their dreams. She gave them encouragement. She believed in them and worked to inspire them. She also supported them financially—as a hardworking and accomplished administrative assistant for a Fortune 500 company in Minneapolis, she had the wherewithal to enable them so that they did not have to get a job (or a life). As Brooke put it, "Isn't it only right to help the man you love get his feet on the ground and get a fresh start toward his dreams?"

As an objective observer watching Brooke's dating history, one might rationally be able to see it for what it was—repeated attempts to enable men who failed to grab hold of the adult responsibilities of life. But for Brooke, her behavior seemed most reasonable. You see, she had grown up the oldest child in her family. Her father was an alcoholic and her mother struggled with depression, and much of the responsibility for keeping the family running smoothly had fallen on Brooke's shoulders. Because of her family of origin, Brooke had grown accustomed to doing for adults what they could (and should) be doing for themselves, and unfortunately, this is what she had mistakenly come to understand as love.[27]

It Just Doesn't Work

> If I am attached to another person because I cannot stand on my own two feet, he or she may be a life saver, but the relationship is not one of love.
>
> Erich Fromm

Each of these relationships ended painfully for Brooke. Despite her best efforts—physical, emotional, and financial—none of these men managed to grab hold of their circumstances and make concrete progress in their lives. Simply put, it just doesn't work—dating a fixer-upper in an effort to give them a life never works. And if you attempt it, as Brooke found out, you are in for a rough ride on the dating tilt-a-whirl. And be warned: if you go ahead and marry such a person, you will in all likelihood end up on the tilt-a-whirl ride of life.

Imagine that you were browsing the classifieds on an Internet dating site and you found the following ad posted by an attractive young man with a chiseled physique: "SWM, great musician, lots of potential, no full-time job for the past two years, plan to pursue a life in music, unmotivated to get permanent work, did a great gig at a local coffee shop recently, not interested in a steady career, expect to be discovered any day now, looking for an attractive woman to enjoy life with."

What do you think? Would you jump at this one? I hope not—at least, not if you are looking for a stable, long-term marriage companion. And yet, way too often, this is exactly what a person says yes to. Within the first few months of being with someone—as if you were reading a dating service personal ad—it is clear whether a person has an interesting and stimulating life, whether they have a network of friends, whether they are going somewhere with their lives, or whether they are in a perpetual holding pattern, undirected and unmotivated, going nowhere fast.

People who have a life have something to bring to a relationship. They don't need you to give their life meaning, purpose, and passion. They already have that. They simply need someone to share it with. But people who don't have a life—except what you manage to give to them—nearly always revert to their previous directionless existence. And in the meantime, they will almost certainly be takers more than givers.

With each of the men Brooke had dated, she saw potential, but it took her way too long to notice that her efforts on their behalf were not being matched by theirs. It is true that we all have potential, but it is important to remember that without concrete goals, objectives, and plans in place, whatever potential we have will not be realized. It will merely remain unlived potential, and as Brooke learned the hard way, dating unlived potential typically does not result in a love that is fruitful and life-giving.

Have You Ever Tried to Nail Jello to a Tree?

> Finding someone who fills an unmet childhood need is often such a relief that a person will stay in an otherwise unrewarding relationship because of fear of losing what has been gained.
>
> Clair Carmichael

A few years ago, there was a young woman here at the university who had been in four of my classes. As a result, I ended up getting to know Mary really well. As a student, Mary was outstanding—she was bright, attentive, hardworking, and diligent. Her exam performances were excellent, her papers were exemplary, and her classroom contributions were always insightful. She was a delight to have in class.

Over the course of the three years in which Mary was a student in these classes, we had several opportunities for conversations outside of class. It was during one of these conversations that Mary first shared with me what she termed "the biggest blow in my entire life." When she was twelve years old, her parents divorced.

Mary had grown up with her mother, father, and two siblings in what appeared to be a strong and stable family. To Mary, there had never been any indication of problems in her parents' marriage. But then one night, her parents sat the three kids down and told them that their father was moving out. He moved the following weekend. As Mary put it, "That night changed my whole life. It was a blow from which I think I am still trying to recover. And even though I still see my father from time to time, it's as if there's a giant hole in my life. He walked out, leaving this big vacuum, and there just hasn't been anything there to fill it."

During her senior year in college, Mary started dating a young man, Ryan, with whom she fell madly in love. Apparently, she had finally met someone to fill that hole. The relationship seemed to start off well for the first few weeks. They spent lots of time together, and they seemed to get along great. But it wasn't long before a pattern of inconsistencies in Ryan's behavior began to emerge. Essentially, Ryan would repeatedly say one thing but then do another. For example, he would promise to meet Mary for lunch in the campus student center, only to "forget." And although Ryan was typically apologetic, his reasons for not showing up were usually quite vague. Or it might be a Friday night, one for which Mary and Ryan had plans together, but then Ryan would call or text (often at the last minute), with the excuse that something had come up and he couldn't make it. And then there were the times Ryan said that he would call, or that he would meet Mary at the library, or that he would come over to her place, and repeatedly he didn't. Like jello to a tree, Ryan was tough to nail down.

Wiser and Stronger

> After you've been hurt, the wrong lesson is "Don't trust again." The right lesson is "Trust wisely."
>
> Mark Goulston

When Mary and Ryan were together, Ryan was kind, undemanding, and attentive. He was pleasant and fun-loving, and he consistently showed Mary the affection she so badly craved. Unfortunately, Ryan was also elusive. He was slippery. Habitually, he would tell Mary one thing and then end up doing something quite different, and in the end, Mary couldn't tell when he would be true to his word and when he wouldn't.[28]

Mary and I had several long talks about her relationship with Ryan. I repeatedly tried to get Mary to see how unpredictable and seemingly untrustworthy Ryan was, but she repeatedly explained away his unreliable behavior. I repeatedly pointed out to Mary how the excuses Ryan so often provided were vague and evasive, but she repeatedly talked about how affectionate he was when they were together. I repeatedly encouraged Mary to heed the (paraphrased) warning from Ralph Waldo Emerson: "What you do shouts so loudly in my ears that I can't hear what you say," but she repeatedly talked about how much she loved him.

In the end, Mary learned the hard way that actions speak louder than words. Ryan was not only elusive, he was also unfaithful—with several women. The news was initially devastating to Mary, but she eventually bounced back. And as she did, she became wiser and stronger than she had ever been before.

Slowly Mary came to realize that she had a big part to play in her own deception. She started to see that her desire to be loved had far outweighed her desire to see Ryan for who he really was. She came to understand just how much she had wanted the hole in her life to be filled—so much so that she was willing to fall for the sweet talk of an untrustworthy man. And over time, she came to the difficult self-discovery that what she had been looking for all along (in the name of love) was really just relief from the pain that had resulted from the loss of her father years earlier.[29]

Ryan's unreliable and cheating behavior had been very difficult for Mary, and her own journey of self-discovery was anything but pleasant. But as Mary put it, "I would do it all over again in order to learn what I came to understand through that extremely painful process. I learned to open my eyes and see what is right in front of me. I learned that seeing things accurately is far more important than relief from personal pain. In fact, I guess you could say that I learned a life lesson through that difficult and painful experience. I learned to value the truth more than consolation, facts more than solace, and reality more than comfort."

Unfortunately, way too many people go from one dating partner to another, repeating the same foolish mistakes, not realizing that there are lessons to be learned from the painful experiences of life. But not Mary. She was reflective. She did not simply blame Ryan and then move on. Instead, she took a cold, hard look at herself, and what she saw was not a pleasant sight. But that did not deter her, and in the end, she developed a determination to keep her eyes wide open in all future dating relationships. Although it took a while, Mary's new approach to dating—don't overlook the obvious—paid off. Mary is now married to a loving, hardworking, reliable, caring, and trustworthy man who is devoted to her and their three children.

Oil and Water

> Life is partly what we make of it, and partly what it is made by the friends we choose.
>
> Tehri Hsieh

There is one question that seems to come up repeatedly. Whether in a class that I'm teaching or in a question-and-answer session following a talk, people want to know: "Is it true that birds of a feather flock together? Or is it the case that opposites attract? When it comes to marriage success, which one is it?"

The bottom line is something like this: avoid extreme differences.[30] For example, imagine that you like things to be in order. Whether it's the routine you follow each day, or your apartment that is regulated by the slogan "a place for everything and everything in its place," or your weekly schedule that is mapped out each Sunday night before you go to bed—you like predictability. But imagine that you meet someone who is highly spontaneous; for him, routine is repugnant, apartment neatness is loathed, and a weekly schedule is abhorred. For this person, chaos seems to be the order of the day. Not a good match.

I know a young couple from two different US cities who met when they were participating in a study-abroad program in Spain. They were like oil and water—she loved order, he loved chaos—but they fell in love. Throughout their time in Spain, what they had in common was that they were both foreigners in a strange land. It was this commonality that overshadowed their blatant differences.

Once they got back to the States, they continued their correspondence via e-mails, texts, and phone calls. And since it is difficult to tell what someone is really like when you don't spend face-to-face time together, they continued to be madly in love with one another. This went on for months, each developing a growing certainty that this was "the one." Finally, after they had been apart for what seemed like an eternity, he came to her home city for a lengthy visit. Before the week was out, it was obvious that oil and water don't mix. Fortunately, they found this out before they did anything foolish, like decide to get married. But even so, it took them over a year to realize something that was obvious from the outset.

Blatant Differences

> Seek those who find your road agreeable, your personality and mind stimulating, your philosophy acceptable, and your experiences helpful.
>
> Jean-Henri Fabre

Typically, when a couple has blatant differences, this does not bode well for the long-term success of the relationship. Jeremy and Meg met while both were serving on a mission trip in El Salvador. Meg was a bright, personable, charismatic, and fun-loving woman. Jeremy, on the other hand, was a little slower to catch on to things, and he preferred to spend his time alone, quietly reading, working on small projects, or browsing the Internet. During the mission trip, Jeremy and Meg fell in love, and they married soon after returning to their homes in Minnesota. From the first weeks of their marriage, Meg tried to get Jeremy to change—to become more engaging, to be sharper intellectually, and to become more outgoing. Needless to say, it didn't work.

Despite Meg's encouragement to change (and Jeremy's desire to do so), he could not become brighter simply because they both wanted him to. Despite his best efforts, he was always going to be intellectually several steps behind Meg. Similarly, Jeremy was never going to become as social and outgoing as Meg had hoped for. Although he worked at it—for example, spending less time alone on the computer and spending more time in social settings—Jeremy was unable to become social enough to keep up with Meg's lively and sociable demeanor.

Do you ever look at a marriage and ask yourself how these two ended up together? Both wonderful people, but blatantly mismatched. That was Jeremy and Meg. Both of them have so much to offer, but they were mismatched. They missed the signs that were blatantly obvious—signs that they should have noticed in the first six months of dating. Jeremy and Meg are still married, but Jeremy constantly feels as though he doesn't quite measure up to Meg's expectations, and Meg often silently concurs, feeling frustrated and disappointed. Jeremy and Meg's relationship has lasted for fifteen years, but as Jeremy quietly told me one day, "It probably should have lasted for fifteen days if we had been willing to see our stark differences."

More Blatant Differences

> We can summarize the research this way: very dissimilar people do not usually marry, and if they do, they are often among the couples who are likely to divorce.
>
> David Olson, John DeFrain, and Linda Skogrand

When we are talking about those blatant differences that can result in serious marital mismatches, we are almost always talking about something that is highly resistant to change. Whether the qualities themselves are resistant to change or the person who possesses them is resistant to change, either way, a thriving future together is doubtful

Ben was a man of seemingly boundless energy. After working a twelve-hour day, he would spend a couple of hours working out, only to be ready for an active evening once he got home. His wife, on the other hand, was a low-energy person. She was typically exhausted by four o'clock and ready for bed by eight o'clock. Ben and his wife stayed together for eight years, even though they should have seen their blatant differences after just eight weeks of dating.

Martha and Tom met on a subway train, and they quickly fell in love, she with a strong faith in God, he an avowed atheist. The differences between them were obvious from the beginning (and not just on Sundays), but their differences seemed to intensify their passion for one another. And the more Martha's parents opposed the relationship, the stronger their passion got. They ended up marrying, a union that ended tumultuously.

Erika had just come off a painful breakup with her long-term boyfriend when she met Connor at her new employer's Christmas party. Connor had been painfully laid off from his dream job, and he was just starting with a new company. Both Erika and Connor, each in their own way, were coming off very difficult personal circumstances. As is often the case, this created a situation that was ripe for mismatched love—each was there for the other to provide solace in the midst of their recent losses. As a result, Erika and Connor dated for quite some time before they began to notice that their core values and life goals were drastically different. For example, Erika wanted to get married much later in life (if at all), she was ambivalent about having children, and her hopes for life amounted to making her first million by the age of thirty, having a lavish home in the country at age thirty-five, and spending at least a month in every country in Europe by the time she was forty. Connor, on the other hand, was looking forward to marriage and having children—the sooner, the better—and what he wanted most out of life was a good home and a loving family to share it with. Erika and Connor dated for three years before they realized how different their core values and life goals were.

A Threefold Cord

> Two are better than one...For if they fall, the one will lift up his fellow...And if one prevail against him, two shall withstand him; and a threefold cord is not easily broken.
>
> Ecclesiastes 4: 9-10, 12

My wife's family is in the twine business, and I spent many long hours as a young adult unloading twine from the bowels of barges docked along the Iowa shores of the Mississippi River. It was then that I first became aware of how thin and frail each strand of twine actually is. Individually, each fiber of rope will give way rather easily, with relatively little strength to withstand a heavy load. But when the individual fibers are woven together, the resulting tenacity is impressive.

So it is with marriage. Better two than one alone. When one falls, the other is there to help. When there is adversity, the two together will be better able to stand firm. But even better is a threefold cord—even better is a marriage where husband and wife are intertwined with God. This is at the heart of successful marriages—a man, a woman, *and* God. A threefold cord is not easily broken.

Many people find it surprising that the evidence deriving from psychological studies confirms this fact. Each semester in the Psychology of Marriage and Family class I teach, students are asked to do a pro/con paper. In other words, based on the psychological research literature, what is the pro-marriage evidence for a particular behavior versus what evidence exists that this behavior undermines marital success? Each semester, someone will want to do this paper on the value of participating in religious services and the importance of a personal connection with God for the success of marriages. I enthusiastically encourage them to do so

Inevitably, within a week or two of researching the topic, the student will come back to tell me: "Dr. Buri, I can't find any negatives. All the research evidence points to the positive effects on marriage of both religious participation and of having a connection with God. Unless I'm missing something, all the evidence seems to be saying that if you want a successful marriage, then you should be religiously active and you should make God an important part of your love for one another." I always reassure them: "You aren't missing anything."[31]

In reality, virtually every study ever done investigating the importance of religion in marital success has confirmed that if you want a long-term, stable, and satisfying marriage, then you should be religiously active and you should make connecting with God a priority in your life. Such consistent findings from empirical research studies often surprise people, but they shouldn't. After all, a primary difference between God and us as human beings is that God loves all the time. It is only reasonable, therefore, that since love is at the heart of every successful marriage, if we want to come closer to loving as God loves—all the time—then getting closer to God will help to make that a reality.

On a Personal Note

> Any person can make a mistake, but only an idiot persists in his error.
>
> Cicero

Unfortunately, I had to find out about the importance of God in marriage the hard way—through personal experience. Kathy and I were high school sweethearts, and we were both active in our churches growing up. This continued during much of the time we were dating, and our relationship thrived.

But for a variety of reasons, we slowly began to move away from God as we were ending our college years and beginning our life together as a married couple. We stopped going to church, and whatever remained of personal time with God ceased for each of us. Within three short years of our wedding day, we found that we had grown miles apart. This woman—the love of my life—was slowly slipping away.

How could we have gone from this couple who so obviously cared about one another to a couple who contemplated splitting? In just a few short years, how could we have grown so far apart? We began to take stock of our lives, looking for something that might hold the key to our failing marriage. Neither of us wanted to go our separate ways. We really did want to recapture the love for each other that we had so clearly experienced before.

As we began to take a serious look at what had changed in our lives, we slowly came to realize that not only had we grown apart from each other, but we had also grown apart from God. We decided to go back to church.

I have to admit—initially it did not go so well. Getting out of bed was not easy, and the church experience was much drier than I had remembered. Furthermore, not much seemed to be happening—neither in our relationship with God nor in our marriage. But as we found out, the problem was not in the church. As Garrison Keillor once poignantly stated, "Going to church no more makes you a Christian than standing in a garage makes you a car." Simply put, we had to do more than simply go to church. We had to actively pursue that Person for whom church exists. We did, and as we did, our love for one another once again came alive.

From personal experience (as well as from a wealth of research evidence), I can tell you that if you want a successful marriage, then go to church. And it isn't enough that we merely be in attendance, but we need to also actively engage him whom we celebrate at church. God is the source—the wellspring—of love, and if we want the love in our marriage to thrive, then we need to connect with that source of love. To the extent that we do, there is hope for that abundant love that we long for in our marriages, for as Gandhi once said, "Where there is love, there is life."

Key No. 3

During the first six months (or so) of dating, one of the biggest choices before us is whether we are going to keep our eyes wide open and actually take discerning stock of the relationship we are in.

- How does your partner treat people?
  - ✓ Are they harsh and unkind?
  - ✓ Are they rude and demanding?
  - ✓ Are they negative and inconsiderate?
  - ✓ Are they gloomy and morose?
  - ✓ The best predictor of future behavior is past behavior. If you want to know how this person will treat you in the future, watch how they respond to different people in their life now.

- Does your partner have a life?
  - ✓ Are they in a perpetual holding pattern, undirected and unmotivated?
  - ✓ Do they have a stimulating life without you?
  - ✓ Do they have a network of friends?
  - ✓ Some people are drawn to unrealized potential in dating partners. They are drawn to the difference they feel they can make in those individuals' lives.
  - ✓ Beware of doing for others what they could (and should) be doing for themselves.
  - ✓ If someone has done little (without your help) to move their life forward, then there is a very good chance that they will do little to move their love forward either.
  - ✓ Don't forget that it takes two to make love work, but only one to make it fail.

- Can you trust this person?
  - ✓ Are they true to their word?
  - ✓ If they say they'll do something, can you count on it getting done?
  - ✓ Have you witnessed this person lying to someone else?
  - ✓ What someone does is a better indicator of who they are than what they say. "What you do shouts so loudly in my ears that I can't hear what you say" (Ralph Waldo Emerson).
  - ✓ Don't simply listen to what someone tells you. Also, watch what they do.
  - ✓ In the end, actions speak louder than words—and this is nowhere more true than in love.

- Are there blatant differences between you?
  - ✓ Is one a neat-freak and the other a slob?
  - ✓ Is one bright, bubbly, and outgoing while the other is dull, quiet, and introverted?
  - ✓ Is one an energetic go-getter while the other is low-energy?
  - ✓ Is one devoutly religious while the other wants nothing to do with God?
  - ✓ Are your core values and life goals drastically different?
  - ✓ Avoid dating someone with blatant differences.
  - ✓ Often the uniqueness of such differences will arouse a sense of novelty and excitement in the relationship. But resist the allure of such attractions. They almost never provide a good foundation for stable, long-term love.

- Find someone who wants to develop an ongoing relationship of love with God.

What Is Dating for, Anyway?

Getting to Know Each Other

> Dating is your opportunity to evaluate the people you meet and develop relationships. Don't use your dates to be entertained.
>
> Margaret Kent

We live in an entertainment age. Whether it's movies or computer games or television or surfing the Internet or sports or music or videos or iPods or texting (you get the idea), we have grown accustomed to being entertained. I am frequently surprised by the number of couples who end up spending almost all their time together during the early months of dating being entertained. Whenever they are together, they end up doing something that entertains them, rather than spending that time simply being together and getting to know one another. How can we ever expect to discern the keys to the First-Six-Months Test if nearly all the time spent together is in the midst of entertainment? How much can I really get to know about someone if nearly all our time together is spent watching sporting events, viewing movies, playing video games, texting friends, and catching reruns of *Seinfeld* and *The Office*?

In the Psychology of Marriage and Family course that I have been teaching for over twenty-five years, each semester I will offer the dating students in the class a little challenge. It goes something like this: "For the next two weeks, when you and your boyfriend (or girlfriend) are together, try to go without any television, movies, videos, or iPhones. See how it goes. See how much the two of you enjoy each other without any of the usual entertainment distractions in your relationship."[32]

I will never forget the semester when a young woman sitting in the middle of the first row excitedly exclaimed: "I can't wait for my boyfriend and me to do this. What an opportunity for communication. Wow, we're going to get to know each other so much better!" The class that semester met once a week, so at the start of class the following week, I asked her how the challenge was going for her and her boyfriend. She sadly stated, "We broke up." She was obviously disappointed. I was not. It was much better that she find out earlier rather than later just how much of a foundation there was for their relationship.

Now, if you really want the ultimate don't-be-entertained-when-together challenge, extend this also to those times when you are riding together in the car. No music. If you try this, and the silence is deafening, then you may have reason to wonder whether the two of you have enough in common to sustain married love. As Oscar Wilde once wrote, "The bond of all companionship, whether in marriage or in friendship, is conversation."

Last semester, a student and her boyfriend tried this latter challenge as they were driving to her hometown, which was two hours away. She reported that their conversation was nonstop throughout both two-hour trips. They found that they had enough commonalities, enough mutual interests, and enough give-and-take that they were able to spend an extended period of time together without being entertained. What a wonderful thing to discover early in a relationship. It should not come as a surprise that their relationship is still going strong.

Key No. 4

Don't use dating simply as an opportunity to be entertained.

Dating is a perfect time to get to know each other. Use it for just that.

Find out if you have enough in common to sincerely enjoy each other's company.

Find out if you can spend extended periods of time together without merely being entertained.

Deer Hunting, Poaching, and Dating

> The idea that love overtakes you is nonsense. This is but a polite manifestation of sex. To love another, you have to undertake some fragment of their destiny.
>
> Quentin Crisp

Deer hunting is a favorite pastime for many people here in Minnesota. Each fall, there are hundreds of men and women out in the woods trying their best to bag a deer. And for some (even though it's illegal), their best entails poaching.

Poaching may involve the placement of highly enticing deer delectables—a feeder dispensing corn, or a field scattered with pumpkins, or a tempting salt lick—so that the unsuspecting prey will get all caught up in the moment and won't notice that they are in a truly unhealthy situation. At other times, poaching might consist of shining a bright light into the eyes of a deer, causing it to freeze. And even though the deer is in a dangerous situation, it won't do anything to remove itself from the danger.

A couple of years ago a young man, Jason, came into my office here at the university. Jason had been in a couple of my classes the previous year, so I knew him quite well. He wanted to talk about his love interest of the past five months. He was really into this young woman, but a recent conversation with his father had him wondering.

This is what Jason told me: "My father and I were talking, and he started asking me about my relationship with Jolene. I knew that my father wasn't very crazy about her, but I wasn't sure exactly why. At the time, I figured that they had simply gotten off on the wrong foot or something. At any rate, as we talked, my father said something that sort of startled me. He said, 'You know, Jason, if the sex with Jolene wasn't so good, then you'd quickly be able to see how truly unhealthy the relationship is.' I was left pretty speechless, but my father didn't miss a beat. He went on to suggest that we simply cool the sex in our relationship for a few weeks, just to see what would happen."

Jason wanted to know what I thought. Was his father nuts? Or did he possibly have a point? We talked about it for a while, and in the end, Jason decided to give it a shot—no sex with Jolene for the next few weeks. They would spend time together, hanging out, going on dates, but no amorous exchanges beyond mild kissing—for the next few weeks!

How Could I Have Been So Stupid?

> One of the more interesting findings of the brain scan studies showed that sexual passion appears to deactivate parts of the brain associated with critical thought...The findings may help explain why people in love often seem to make bad decisions.
>
> Tara Parker-Pope

About two weeks into this little experiment, Jason came wandering into my office one morning. "I need to talk with you," he said dejectedly. "I don't know how I could have been so stupid. Jolene is one of the most sullen, depressing, sad-sack people I have ever met. The first night we went out, she pouted when they didn't have tofu on the menu, and then she brooded during the whole meal because I didn't want to leave and go someplace else. She ended up spending the whole night all moody and depressed. Over what—no tofu?

"At first, I thought that maybe this was an unusual night—you know, that time of the month or something—but over the next week or so, I began to realize that this stuff is not unusual. In fact, I slowly began to realize that this is the way she is most of the time. She's nearly always gloomy and pessimistic—whether it's that her clothes don't fit her well enough or that the weather's not sunny enough or her roommate's not friendly enough or her mother doesn't call enough—she sulks and pouts, and she wants to pull everyone down with her. In fact, if you don't become moody and dejected with her, then she doesn't think you care about her. How could I have missed it? How could I have been so stupid?"

How could Jason have missed it? One obvious answer can be found in the biochemical love potion (e.g., dopamine, norepinephrine, phenylethylamine) whirling around in the brain that we discussed in chapter 2. Functional magnetic resonance imaging (fMRI) studies have revealed that sex serves to increase the presence of these chemicals in the brain, stirring them into a powerful love brew and heating it up to a sometimes feverish pitch. And when this happens, those areas of the brain responsible for critical reasoning and healthy judgment are suppressed.[33] Literally, we are in a drug-induced state. And once this has occurred, the brain is less responsive to those behaviors that are right in front of our noses and would otherwise be obvious. We end up like the poached deer, finding it difficult to detect the truly unhealthy situation in which we may find ourselves.

Key No. 5

> When it comes to seeing the potential problem behaviors in a dating partner, nothing interferes with that awareness quite like sex.
>
> Sex blinds us like nothing else in the dating process. Once the entertainment has moved from the living room into the bedroom, then problem behaviors become almost impossible to notice.
>
> If you want to find healthy long-term love, go easy on your sexual involvement—it will interfere with your capacity to choose wisely.

Several population-based studies have revealed that not only does premarital sexual behavior run the risk of blurring one's ability to notice problem behaviors, but it also increases the risk of divorce once people do marry. For example, in one study involving over ten thousand young adults, having just one nonmarital sexual partner besides your spouse was associated with a 300 percent greater chance of divorce.[34] When we let what is happening between our legs overpower that which is happening between our ears, seldom does anything good come from it.

Some readers may be surprised to find that the number of young adults not having sex is actually on the rise. The latest statistics generated by the National Survey of Family Growth revealed that nearly 33 percent of young women and over 25 percent of young men reported no sexual behavior with another person.[35] Even in a seductive, sex-saturated culture, it is possible to keep your wits about you, and a growing number of young women and men are doing just that.

Marriage Tour Guide

> When a person's knowledge is not in order, the more of it he has, the greater will be his confusion.
>
> Herbert Spencer

In each of us there is a desire to love and to be loved. It is part of our nature. It is part of who we are as human beings.[36] That longing for this type of intimacy is met nowhere else like it is in marriage. In fact, marriage is uniquely designed to meet these desires. Furthermore, the fact that 96 percent of Americans say that they have a strong desire to marry[37] belies the fact that most of us (at least, intuitively) understand this reality.

And yet, the way we do dating does not mirror this desire. In the Psychology of Marriage and Family course I teach, we spend a lot of time talking about what marriage is like—the typical highs and lows in marriage, the transitions in married life that can be expected, some of the pitfalls to watch out for, behavior patterns to avoid, why marriages fail, and how to make the most of your marriage opportunity. It is a very popular course, consistently filled to capacity. I love teaching the course, but I often have this odd experience while teaching it. It's as if I'm a tour guide to a strange land for a group of prospective travelers whose trip to this novel place is still many years away.

Let me explain. Imagine that you're planning a trip to South Africa, and even though you have no intention of going there anytime soon, you decide to take a class from someone who can give you a good idea of what visiting this new country will be like. You would probably take the course, gathering the information with sort of an ambivalent distance, with an attitude that says something like: "Interesting. I'll have to remember this information someday—when it might actually be relevant."

That's what it's like teaching young adults about marriage: "Interesting, but this is not at all relevant to where I'm at in my life right now." This perspective was poignantly captured recently in a question asked by a young woman is class: "Dr. Buri, when should people stop dating for fun and start dating for marriage?"

I know that for many people such a question does not seem strange at all, but for me, it's very strange. Think about it. We have essentially spawned a dating culture in which what we are doing is in many ways unrelated to the end toward which we are motivated. The very things that often make for an enjoyable in-loveness dating relationship—spontaneity, novelty, excitement, romance—are not the primary things that make for a good marriage. Don't get me wrong. Marriages need spontaneity, novelty, excitement, and romance, but even in the best of them, you end up with more predictability than spontaneity, more familiarity than novelty, more ordinariness than excitement, and more routine than romance. Unfortunately, what most of us as young adults end up doing is spending years of our dating lives preparing not for marriage, but rather, preparing for more years of dating. Is it any wonder, then, that a sizable number of men and women end up marrying, only to find themselves unmarrying and again entering the world of dating?

I was recently engaged in a conversation with a group of new college graduates, and to a person, they all agreed that they would not be getting married anytime soon, and most of them intended to forestall the inevitable until well into their thirties.[38] In the meantime, as they explained, they had "a lot of living to do." Somehow, we seem to have settled on the conviction that married life is the antithesis of living—"once I'm ready to settle down, then I'll get married, but in the meantime, I have a lot of living to do." But in reality, nothing could be further from the truth. When marriage is done well, living is enriched, not thwarted. Our lives unfold and take shape in a way that no other experience can affect. When we do marriage well—when we find a good traveling companion on this journey called life and we love and are loved in return—life is anything but a ball-and-chain experience. Rather, it is an incredibly liberating and life-giving one.

What Had We Been Doing?

> The future is not something we enter. The future is something we create.
>
> Leonard Sweet

"Heartbreak is born of experience." This is how one woman, Denise, described her notion of love. "Derek and I started dating at the end of our freshman year in college," Denise told me, "and we dated for the next three years. When we graduated, I was ready for the next step—marriage. But the more I wanted to talk about marriage, the more Derek pulled away, until one day he told me it was over.

"Needless to say, I was stunned. What had we been doing for the past three years? We seemed to have everything going for us, and then suddenly, it was over. What had we been preparing for—more dating? Until when? I don't want to say I'm jaded about love, but I am certainly more cautious. For me, I guess the bottom line is this: if what Derek and I were doing wasn't leading to marriage, why were we doing it? What was it all about anyway? One thing for sure: I'm never going to get blindsided like that again."

Denise's experience is not unique, except for possibly the length of it. I hear the same story over and over again each semester. The names and details change, but the story line remains pretty much the same. "Boy meets girl. They fall in love. They give as much of themselves to each other as they possibly can. They break up. Both walk away, knowing the pain of a failed attempt at love." Let's face it: the way we do dating is leaving a trail of in-love's walking wounded. When we encourage a depth of giving—personally, emotionally, and physically—of one person to another, but there is no promise of permanence, we are inviting scar tissue on the heart.

I don't want to sound heartless here, because I really was sympathetic to Denise, and I really am sympathetic to all those who have been wounded through their dating experiences—I do understand the hurt and heartache that people have endured in the name of love. But in reality, Denise should have been aware of the blatant differences between her and Derek in terms of their core values and life goals. She should have seen these differences long before Derek walked out of the relationship.

Denise ended up moving on with her life, so I haven't seen her for several years, but my hope is this. Denise told me that she was "never going to get blindsided like that again." My hope is that Denise has not given up on authentic love, and that she has not allowed her heart to become so hardened that she has relinquished her ideals—to love and to be loved. Further, my hope for Denise is that she has learned from this painful life lesson with Derek, that her dating eyes have been opened wide by the experience, and that, as a result, she is now more wise and discerning. Finally, my hope for Denise is that she has found what we all desire—to love and to be loved—and not just for a short-time, but for a lifetime.

Why Wait?

> There is a time when we must firmly choose the course we will follow, or the relentless drift of events will make the decision for us.
>
> Herbert Prochnow

A couple of months ago, I had a conversation with a young woman named Ashley. She is a former student who is now twenty-nine. When Ashley was in college, she had dated a man, Trent, whom she described as "the love of my life." As Ashley put it: "Trent and I got along great. We had chemistry. We could talk for hours. Or we could just hang out, perfectly comfortable in simply being together, saying almost nothing. We never seemed to be at a loss for things that we enjoyed doing together. And it stayed that way for almost three years."

As I listened to Ashley, I thought: "Wow, she had found someone with whom she connected really well. They had chemistry. They were able to communicate. They enjoyed each other's company. The relationship had shown staying power (thriving for nearly three years). What could be better?"

But as Ashley went on, it became clear why she wanted to talk with me. "I think I blew it," she said. "I think I let a truly wonderful man get away. At the time, Trent talked about the two of us getting married, but I wanted no part of it. I wasn't interested in making such a big decision. Besides, I had plans for my life—a career, more education, and (quite honestly) dating other guys. Well, I've had the chance to date a lot of men since Trent, some more seriously, most less so. But I haven't found anyone quite like Trent. I think I blew it. I think I missed out on a really good man."

I wish I could say that Ashley's situation is unique—that very few people begin to think after breaking up that they've blown it, that they've passed on a person who would have made a great life companion. But unfortunately, I can't; I've heard it dozens of times. Way too many men and women want to go out and experience life—not *with* a spouse, but *prior to* a spouse—only to realize (almost always too late) that they let a really good partner get away.

Oftentimes you hear people citing studies suggesting that age at marriage and marital success are inversely related; in other words, the earlier you marry, the less likely you are to experience a successful marriage. As a result, many have been led to believe that the longer you wait to marry, the better. But the truth is that these statistics only apply to age twenty-two and younger. After that, they no longer hold true. In fact, there is recent evidence (based upon a sample of nearly twenty thousand couples) that waiting longer to marry (for example, into your late twenties and early thirties) may actually reduce your chances for a satisfying marriage. As many of us are aware, the older people get, the more set in their ways they become—a trait that is not conducive to the type of give-and-take upon which healthy marriages are built.[39]

Ashley and I talked for quite a while that day, not because I had the answers she was looking for, but because she needed to talk about the pain of a lost love. As I sadly gave her a hug good-bye, I silently wondered: "Why wait? If a person has found someone who would make a wonderful traveling companion on a great adventure, then why not seize the opportunity and make it official? Why not marry that person? Why wait?"

Love Requires Choices

> For most people, a life lived alone, with passing strangers or passing lovers, is incoherent and ultimately unbearable. Someone must be there to know what we have done for those we love.
>
> Frank Pittman

There is nothing in your life that will influence your happiness and life satisfaction more than choosing your spouse. Such decisions do not come easily, and they certainly do not simply befall us. Love requires that we choose. In-loveness may not, but love does. Love always involves choices, and the best choices are made when they are grounded in a reasonable and thoughtful awareness.

I remember as a child being told not to touch the hot stove. Did I listen? No. But I did experience one-trial learning. I have two wishes for dating men and women. First: may we not have to learn the hard lessons of inauthentic love through experience. But unfortunately, most of us do. Therefore, my second wish: may we have many more cases of one-trial learning. Why do we have to get dragged through so many destructive dating experiences, and then still have so little wisdom to show for it?

It is crucial that we see love as a series of choices. And it is vital that we come to understand that the best choices, even in love, are made mindfully and sensibly. If we don't, we will continue to have difficulty discriminating the healthy from the unhealthy, the constructive from the destructive, the reasonable from the unreasonable, and the adaptive from the maladaptive in our dating experiences.

Key No. 6

When is the best time to stop dating for fun and to start dating for marriage?

The sooner, the better.

Possibly now.

We Give Power to Those We Love

Fireworks on the Fourth of July

> Courtship—the period before marriage where people play roles for which they have no use afterwards.
>
> Evan Esar

When asked, "What do most people do on a first date?" Martin (age ten) replied: "On the first date, they just tell each other lies, and that usually gets them interested enough to go for a second date." Although funny, Martin's statement is also true; only ten, he already understands how dating works. Studies have revealed that there is more deception in the world of dating than in any other social context in our culture.[40]

For most people, this deception is exercised in an attempt to put their best foot forward. As Martin so astutely observed, you want to get your partner "interested enough to go for a second date." But for some men and women, the deception in dating is not just a temporary guise, but rather, it is a way of life. We are talking here about the narcissist.

Narcissists come in all shapes, sizes, colors, and ages. Although they can be women, it is estimated that approximately 75 percent of narcissists are men. But regardless of the package, all narcissists have the following in common. They are self-centered, selfish, and self-absorbed. They believe that they are unique and special—more talented, more intelligent, more attractive, more powerful than others—and as such, they feel a sense of entitlement. For example, narcissists are more apt to agree with statements like: "I demand the best because I'm worth it" and "If I were on the Titanic, I would deserve to be on the first lifeboat."[41] Deep down, narcissists really do believe that they are pretty awesome people. Furthermore, narcissists lack the ability to develop caring, empathetic, and loving relationships. Essentially, they don't experience genuine concern for anyone—except themselves.

Why, then, would anyone date such a person (much less marry them)? What is appealing about an egotistical, entitled, uncaring jerk (or jerkette)? The problem is that narcissists wear masks. Love to them is little more than a giant masquerade. For example, on the surface they will often exude charm and interest. They are masters at flattery, telling you what you want to hear. As a result, they often come across as caring. They are confident and they love being the center of attention, so they are often fun and exciting to be with. And in the end, a person can get caught up in the spell of the narcissist, falling prey to the special way in which you feel when they express an interest in you.

I guess you could say that narcissists are something like fireworks on the Fourth of July. They catch your attention, they are alluring and exciting, and they are fun to be around. How many of us don't enjoy fireworks on the Fourth of July? The problem is that narcissists are similar to fireworks in another way as well; if you get too close, you will get burned, and burned badly.

Of Epidemic Proportions

> The rise in narcissism is accelerating, rising faster in the 2000s than in previous generations...Over the last few decades, narcissism has risen as much as obesity... It has spread through the generations like a particularly pernicious virus.
>
> Jean Twenge and W. Keith Campbell

Tiffany met Brandon one night when she was at a friend's house for a party. He immediately caught her eye as he was entertaining several people, regaling one story after another. He was moderately good looking, but he carried himself in a way that magnified his physical attractiveness. When Brandon noticed Tiffany from across the room, his gaze held hers for a couple of seconds. She was smitten. Before the night was out, Tiffany and Brandon had spent close to two hours together. Tiffany remembers being struck by how easy he was to be with. Not only that, but he had noticed her, and he took an interest in her. Needless to say, she was flattered. Furthermore, he was charming, humorous, and engaging. She definitely wanted to see him again.

Jaina was beautiful, not in an unapproachable actress sort of way, but more like that pretty girl in your high school geometry class that made heads turn every time she walked into a room. She had that "wow factor." Jaina was also quite sensual, but she carried it in a way that made her more attractive than seductive, more alluring than slutty. Furthermore, Jaina had a way of making people feel good. She would turn on her beauty and her charm, and people would be captivated. And that is what happened to Bill—he was captivated. He met Jaina through mutual friends and they hit it off immediately. Bill was taken by her alluring beauty and her captivating charm.

Both Brandon and Jaina are narcissists, and both Tiffany and Bill got sucked into the vortex that can so easily happen when you date a narcissist. Neither Tiffany nor Bill remembers exactly when things started to go sour in their relationships with Brandon and Jaina, but both of them wish that they had noticed the telltale signs long before they did. It would have saved both of them a tremendous amount of pain, disappointment, frustration, confusion, and heartache.

The probability that you will experience what Tiffany and Bill did—dating a narcissist—is definitely on the rise. Let me explain. The way in which narcissism is typically measured is with a questionnaire called the Narcissistic Personality Inventory. This questionnaire was developed in the 1980s, and it has been used in a variety of empirical studies since then. By reviewing the results of these studies (involving over sixteen thousand young men and women), we are able to determine the prevalence of narcissism since the 1980s. I doubt that it would surprise anyone to discover that narcissism is on the rise. But what may surprise you is the extent of this increase. Two-thirds of young men and women today score above the original average from the early 1980s. This is an increase of 30 percent in less than three decades.[42]

You and the Narcissist's Allure

> The person who knows others is learned. The person who knows himself is wise.
>
> Lao-tzu

Falling in love with a narcissist is an emotionally fatal attraction. Like being in love with a vampire, such a relationship will end up sucking the life right out of you. Obviously, therefore, the sooner you can pick up on the red flags of narcissism (and begin to look behind the masks narcissists wear), the less pain and misery you are going to end up enduring.

But be aware from the outset: even though many of these warning signs are quite obvious (even noticeable within the first few weeks of dating), narcissists are masters at deception. Furthermore, you may be one of those individuals who are especially vulnerable to the shrewdness of the narcissist. For example, are you someone who believes that love is something that befalls us? In other words, have you been enticed by the Romantic Love Complex? If yes, then you are especially vulnerable to the allure of the narcissist. Similarly, genuinely good-hearted people—those who believe that deep down, people are well-intentioned—are more apt to fall prey to the deceptiveness of the narcissist. Such men and women tend to believe that the vast majority of people are kind and good, and can therefore be trusted. This is a naïve and often dangerous assumption when dealing with narcissists, and such a belief will leave you highly susceptible to their cunning. Finally, if you struggle with low self-esteem, you will be especially receptive to the narcissist's charm and flattery. Like a person dying from thirst in a desert, a pool of skuzzy water might appear better than no water at all, but in fact, it nearly always carries lots of diseases with it.[43]

It probably doesn't need to be stated, but I will go ahead and say it anyway. It is possible for someone to have more than one of these narcissist vulnerabilities. In addition, the more of these you have, the more vulnerable you are. For example, if you are a good-hearted person who is seeking to be in love, then you are a narcissist's easy prey, ripe for the picking. And if you are a good-hearted person with low self-esteem who is looking for in-loveness, then you are the narcissist's trifecta. If these categorizations apply to you, then know that you are especially vulnerable to the deceptiveness of the narcissist. Also know that you will need to work extra hard to pick up on the red flags that are waving (although sometimes subtly) right in front of the narcissist's face.

Warning Signs of a Toxic Partner

> The word narcissism comes from the Greek myth of Narcissus, an attractive young man who set out looking for someone to love. Narcissus keeps looking for the perfect mate until one day he sees his own reflection in the water. Narcissus falls in love with his own image and gazes at it until he dies. The myth of Narcissus captures the tragedy of the person frozen by his own self-admiration and unable to connect with anyone outside of himself.
>
> Jean Twenge and W. Keith Campbell

There are several common warning signs that are part of the narcissistic package.[44] If you see one of these, don't necessarily jump to the conclusion that what you are dealing with is a narcissist. But on the other hand, don't overlook it either. Rather, take this one warning sign as a prod, causing you to be more alert, watching for any other signs that might give away this person's true intent.

No genuine curiosity about you: Narcissists are inclined to talk about themselves—a lot. Although it can sometimes be subtle, narcissists like to boast and brag. They can be masters at redirecting conversations so that what they know, how talented they are, who they've rubbed shoulders with, and where they've been will become obvious for all to see. You might even be talking about something very important to you, but they will exude a hardly-listening, glazed-over look, or they will end up making the conversation more about them than about you. For example, you might be talking about a confrontation you had with a coworker, and before you know it, the conversation has shifted to the narcissist's previous negative work experiences (and how brilliantly they handled them). This is one of the earliest warning signs—narcissists give themselves away in their conversations.

Reactions when challenged: Narcissists expect to be respected. In their self-centered world view, it isn't reasonable that anyone would challenge them. After all, people should understand how talented they are, how much they know, and how many connections they have. So what happens when someone challenges the fact that the narcissist may not know quite as much as they think? What happens when someone points out a shortcoming? Watch the reaction. It is another telltale sign. It is often referred to as the Dr. Jekyll/Mr. Hyde syndrome. Do they get hurt or offended—as if a personal transgression has occurred? Are they annoyed or angry—as if a travesty of justice has happened?

It might even be a tiny thing. You might make the simple observation that you were surprised that they didn't know a question in the Trivial Pursuit game you were playing, and they will interpret your innocent comment as criticism, responding with an indignant overreaction. And beware the trap that has ensnared many women and men—making excuses for the extreme reactions of narcissists: "Oh, he's just under a lot of pressure right now." You don't want to overlook such reactions, and if they are frequent, you want to take note of the giant neon sign flashing. Narcissists cannot be trusted, and if you stay in a relationship with a narcissist, you will get hurt.

Treatment of people in the service industry: A young man recently told me about his first date with a woman he had gotten to know at work. They had gone to a popular Italian restaurant in Minneapolis, and as he told it, this is what happened: "First, she yelled at the valet for taking too long to come park our car, then she chewed out the hostess because our table wasn't ready at the time of our reservation, and then she lit into our waitress because the table had some crumbs on it." Unfortunately, this young man came to talk with me after over a year of dating this woman. The advice I gave him after he was with her for a year would have been the same after just one date. "Watch how she treats the hired help. This will give you a clear indication as to what she's made of." After his first date with this woman, he should have seen enough to start reconsidering the relationship.

More Warning Signs

> I have often wished I had time to cultivate modesty...But I am too busy thinking about myself.
>
> Edith Sitwell

Control: Narcissists expect to be in charge. In fact, they think it's only reasonable that they be in control. For example, one of the items on the Narcissistic Personality Inventory states: "If I ruled the world, it would be a much better place." Narcissists are much more apt to endorse this statement than are other men and women. Think about it for a moment. If narcissists are convinced that the *world* would be a better place if they were in charge, then they certainly are going to believe that *you* (as well as *your relationship*) are going to be better off with them at the helm. Therefore, they are intent upon being in control.

Initially, this in-charge-ness will often get expressed as some form of persuasion. Charm, flattery, and mild emotional pressure can do wonders to melt resistance. It can even be quite subtle. For example, you might say, "I was planning to go out with friends tonight." To which he responds, "Gee, I was hoping that we could be together tonight. I thought you'd want to be with me as much as I want to be with you." Naturally it's flattering to be so desirable that someone wants to spend time with you, but just know that what's going on here is not about love. Narcissists wear masks, and what is masquerading as love is really about control. And unfortunately, if you stay in the relationship long enough, that control will in all likelihood take the form of overt coercion in addition to mild persuasion.

I had a conversation one day after class with a young man who tried to explain what it was like dating his girlfriend of two years.

He put it this way: "Sometimes she will be absolutely wonderful to be with. She'll be warm and affectionate, lavishing me with attention and gentleness. For example, we'll be studying and she'll rub my back or stroke my leg. She just showers me with affection. But then the next day, it's as if the rug has been pulled out from under me. *Woof*, it's all gone, and I'm left trying to figure out what happened. And then I end up doing all sorts of things to have another day like the previous one. But nothing seems to work. No matter how hard I try to please her, to do things for her, to get her to be warm and affectionate, nothing I do seems to make any difference."

What advice would you give this young man? My advice was something like this: "If you are dating someone who turns their emotions on and off like a water faucet, using them at their whim and fancy (at your expense), what is happening in the relationship is not about love. There may be moments of warmth and affection, but don't mistake that for love; it's actually more about control than it is about love. If you respect yourself, seriously consider getting out of the relationship." Judging from this young man's somewhat hasty and huffy exit from my office, I think he decided to leave the conversation rather than leave the relationship.

The Blame Game: Watch for blaming. Narcissists have a strong need to be right. After all, in their minds they are more intelligent, more talented, and more gifted than others, so it is only natural that they would also be more right. So watch for whether they make excuses and fault others for their failings. Watch to see if they build themselves up, often at the expense of someone else. Watch to see if they repeatedly justify their behaviors. Basically, watch to see if they play the blame game. And pay special attention to what is said about former dating partners. Often, the blame that is put on a former partner will make you feel great right now; for example, he may say, "You are so smart, sensitive, and caring, not at all like that shrew I used to go out with." But in the long run, that blame will come around to you. Never forget the Law of

Blame: blame will always (eventually) fall on the people closest to the blamer.

Cupid and the Choices We Make

> Marriage is like a three-speed gear box: affection, friendship, and love. It isn't advisable to crash your gears and go right through to love. You need to ease your way through. The basis of love is respect, and that needs to be learned from affection and friendship.
>
> Peter Ustinov

A common cultural injunctive of love has asserted that there is little one can do in the wake of Cupid's wily arrows. Once struck, it is futile to resist. For example, once you have been smitten by her glance, or bewitched by his charm, or enthralled by her beauty, or wooed by his flattery, or enticed by her sizzle, attempts to resist such frequent fruits of Cupid's arrows will only be met with frustration. So we might as well just go with the flow of love's bidding. What else can we do? That's just the way love is.

But in fact, love is not something that simply happens to us. We are not simply the witless pawns of Cupid's antics. But rather, love is the result of the choices we make. Admittedly, I have moments when I can understand the appeal of clinging to a Cupid view of love. After all, such a view lessens the burden of personal responsibility one needs to embrace as we look at the state of our love lives. Simply put, it is much easier to think of love as something we fall into (or out of) than to seriously consider the burden of responsibility for love that is rightfully ours. It is much easier to think that when it comes to love, we are the innocent beneficiaries—or in the case of dating a narcissist, the innocent victims—of an irresistible force that has overtaken us. So I do understand. As in nearly every other area of life, lessened responsibility lures us with the promise of an easier life.

But this simply isn't true. It's a trap. Life is not easy—or should I say, a fruitful life is not easy. And love is not easy—at least, a fruitful love is not easy.

No, in the end, love comes down to the choices we make. While a Cupid view of love holds out an alluring promise of easy and fulfilling love, it nearly always ends with the reality of a painful and unfulfilling relationship. Love is no different than the rest of life; we normally end up getting that for which we have chosen.

So if you have come to realize that you are dating a narcissist, choose to get out. Don't walk—run. Leave the relationship, and the sooner, the better. If you are tempted to think that you are going to somehow be able to say or do something that will bring about a change in this person, save yourself the misery. Choose to resist this futile temptation. Narcissists are notoriously poor bets for successful relationships, and your hoped-for change in them is not going to happen simply because of your love.

If you are not dating a narcissist, then choose to heed the warning signs. Be aware of them early in a relationship. Chances are—given the epidemic increase in narcissism we are witnessing in our culture—you are going to encounter narcissists in your dating experience. It is doubtful that you will be able to avoid them altogether. But whether or not you fall for their deceits, you can choose. Furthermore, if you are one of those individuals who is especially vulnerable to the allure of the narcissist—for example, if you love to be in love, if you easily trust the good will of others, and/or if you have low self-esteem—then choose to do what is necessary to develop a more healthy and realistic view of love, of human nature, and of yourself.

One further suggestion: the next time you meet a genuinely nice man or woman, choose to give them a little extra time and consideration. They may not have all the charm and polished glitz of the narcissist, but choose nonetheless to give them special attention. In the end, those we love have a unique power to influence how we feel about life and about ourselves. Choose wisely. Genuinely good-hearted people are much more apt to exercise that power for the better. In their hands, we are much more likely to feel good about life and about ourselves.

Key No. 7

Beware the narcissist!

Instead, turn your attention to the genuinely good-hearted person.

In the hands of such a person, your love is much more apt to be safe.

With such a person, you are more apt to thrive.

Narcissism's First Cousin

Are You Headed for a Shipwreck?

> Love is what is left over in a relationship after all the selfishness is taken out.
>
> Nick Richardson

Without a doubt, narcissism is toxic to marriage. The person who marries a narcissist is headed for an unstable and unsatisfying marital union. But there is another quality that people can sometimes take with them into marriage—a quality similar to narcissism in some ways (a first cousin, if you will)—that also takes its toll on marital happiness. This first cousin of narcissism is selfishness.[45]

Numerous authors have made it clear: the most successful marriages are those in which both the husband and the wife approach their life together with a desire to put their partner's needs, desires, and interests above their own.[46] When this is the case, the couple has the makings of a smooth-sailing vessel in which to make their journey on the sea of married love. Obviously, this does not mean that the couple's journey will be without some storms. In fact, I would be willing to bet that they will experience lots of storms, and in all likelihood, some large ones. But what it does mean is that this couple will be working to establish one of the greatest assurances that their marriage vessel will be seaworthy—mutual self-sacrifice for the good of the other.

But what happens if one partner has the desire to put their spouse's needs above their own, but the other partner is mired in a mind-set of self-interest and self-satisfaction? I doubt that this will surprise anyone, but such a marital arrangement just doesn't work very well. When this is the case, it is as if the couple has set sail with an anchor tossed overboard. It will be anything but smooth sailing. The resulting drag on their marriage will day after day encumber their progress toward the marital happiness they so clearly espoused on that day when they said "I do." And if neither partner has a desire to put the welfare of their spouse above their own, then they should prepare themselves for a shipwreck.

We-ness

> Successful marriages are woven out of many strands of inhibited desire—the deferment to the wishes of the other; acceptance of infringements on one's own wishes; disappointments swallowed; confrontations avoided; opportunities for anger bypassed; chances for self-expression muted. To introduce selfishness into this process is to take a broomstick to a delicate web.
>
> Daniel Yankelovitch

About twenty years ago, a new term popped up in the marriage and family literature. The first time I saw this term, it had a jolting effect on me. It was both confusing and enlightening, perplexing and illuminating, puzzling and clarifying. The term is *we-ness*, and over the past twenty years, it has become more and more obvious to many marriage therapists, educators, authors, and researchers that we-ness is a vital key to successful, stable, and happy marriages.[47]

In a nutshell, we-ness is two *me*'s becoming a *we*. It entails repeatedly putting *we* before *me*. One couple I know has a carved wooden sign that graces the entrance to their home. The sign reads: "As for me, *we* comes first." When both partners embrace a slogan like this, you can expect wonderful things to happen in their marriage.

The beauty of the term we-ness is that it flies in the face of the technocratic culture in which we find ourselves. In more and more contexts, we are led to believe that all one need do to accomplish a desired goal is to follow a prescribed procedure—follow this foolproof technique and success will be yours. For example, as parents we are told: "If you want to change your child's behavior, just follow this straightforward approach." Or in business, we are encouraged: "Just follow these steps to increase your client base and your revenue." Over and over again, we are told that all we need to do is follow a simple step-by-step procedure to lose weight, to boost your energy, to increase your return on investments, to improve your health, to prolong your life, to maximize your happiness, or to change your marriage.

But as many people can attest, a loving and life-giving marriage cannot be accomplished by simply following a set of prearranged techniques. For example, several years ago I was working with a husband who asked, "How do you let your wife know that you love her?" We talked about this for quite a while, and when we were finished, he was determined to go home and do some of these things to let his wife know he loved her.

The next time I saw this man, I asked him how it was going. He explained that he had purchased some flowers because his wife really likes flowers, that he had brought home some candy because his wife really likes candy, that he had said "those three little words" because his wife really likes to hear them, and that he had taken her out on a date for their anniversary because that is what is expected of loving husbands. Maybe you can imagine his wife's response. She bluntly stated: "I don't want you to *do* the things a loving husband does, like some sort of robot that has been preprogrammed. I want you to *be* a loving husband."

We-ness and Selfishness

> Love is, above all, the gift of oneself.
>
> Jean Anouilh

We are being taught to be technocrats. "Tell me what to do and I'll do it." "Show me the steps to follow and I'll follow them to the letter." "Just help me understand the technique and I'll get it down, and then we'll be fine." Admittedly, this often works well in a computerized age. With computers, if you are given procedures to follow, or techniques to implement, or step-by-step instructions to carry out, then the results are typically quite straightforward and effective. The problem is that loving relationships don't work like computers. You can't simply program two *me*'s to become a *we*. There is no cut-and-dried procedure that guarantees a growing closeness and connectedness between me-1 and me-2. We-ness can't simply be accomplished by pushing a few buttons of a computer program. Instead, we-ness is accomplished when each partner asks over and over again: "What can I do in this situation for the sake of *we* rather than for the sake of *me*."

This brings us back to selfishness. Obviously, if one spouse struggles to put their partner's needs, desires, and interests on a level equal to their own, then the probability of we-ness between that couple is practically nil. Certainly, one spouse can day after day exercise decisions toward we-ness in the marriage, but without a partner who participates equally in this process, these efforts will nearly always result in aggravation, exasperation, frustration, and exhaustion (not to mention very limited movement toward the goal of we-ness).

Take, for example, Marni and Phil, who had been married for a little over eight years when I first met them. At the heart of their failing marriage was the fact that Marni could not count on Phil for consistent help around the house. This situation had come to a head when they had their first baby three years earlier. After having the baby, even though Marni had returned to full-time work outside the home, she was still unable to rely on Phil's help around the house. He would occasionally take out the garbage or mow the lawn, but his participation in the household tasks did not go much beyond that. And when Marni did sometimes ask Phil for help with other tasks, he would typically do them, but never without an attitude of being put out. To make things even more frustrating for Marni, Phil would repeatedly come home late from work without letting her know that he was going to be late, or he would go out with friends without first talking with her.

Needless to say, Phil had a poor sense of we-ness. He had grown up an only child, and his parents had divorced when he was nine. As a result, he spent his teen years on his own for much of the time, and only occasionally was he expected to let his mother know his whereabouts. Essentially, he was accustomed to coming and going pretty much as he pleased. Furthermore, since he was involved in numerous activities at school, he was only rarely expected to do anything around the house to help support the family.

It was not the case that Phil was undisciplined or irresponsible during his growing up years. On the contrary, he showed considerable self-discipline and responsibility. However, these traits were almost always exercised in the pursuit of his own personal self-interests. He had never been asked to think about how his actions might impact someone close to him. He had never been trained to ask himself the question: "If I decide to do this, how will that decision affect anyone else?" As a result, *we* was not at the forefront of his consciousness as he went through his day-to-day activities. And as Marni found out, cajoling, pleading, prodding, and nagging did not do anything to create the desired sense of we-ness in Phil's consciousness. In fact (as many have discovered), it only made things worse.

Relationship Maintenance and Selfishness

> Happiness is not so much in having as in sharing. We make a living by what we get, but we make a life by what we give.
>
> Norman MacEwan

Have you ever thought about how much work goes into sustaining and nurturing the love you have for someone? During the early stages of being in love, it may feel like this love for them is effortless and that it happens spontaneously, but in reality, you are putting quite a bit of work into it. For example, you think about that person, you look forward to being with them, you plan your next time together, you find areas of common enjoyment, and when you are together, you focus intently on that person. Essentially, when we love, we work at understanding, appreciating, and satisfying the needs, desires, and interests of the one we love. For psychologists, this is called relationship maintenance.[48]

If you want a successful long-term marriage, then you will have to sustain and nurture your love—even after the initial in-loveness has begun to wane. In other words, if you want love to be at the center of your marriage, you will have to work at relationship maintenance. Even after the effortlessness of in-loveness has worn off, you will have to work at thinking about your spouse, looking forward to being with them, planning your next time together, finding areas of common enjoyment, and when you are together, focusing intently on them. Simply put, any couple that desires a long-term loving relationship needs to be committed to the ongoing work of understanding, appreciating, and satisfying the needs, desires, and interests of the one they love.

As you might suspect, this is not an easy charge for any of us. It is not as if all the other demands of life—work responsibilities, bills, car and home upkeep, children—simply stop so that we can focus on the relationship maintenance that is so essential to our married love. Unfortunately, this is not the way life works. Instead, we must learn how to sustain and nurture our love while at the same time satisfying the many other demands of life. I wish I could tell you that love just keeps coming—that it's not work, and that it continues to flow freely with little attention or effort on our part—but the truth is that in virtually every area of life, we are not going to get more out of something than we have put into it. It's the same with love. We are not going to get more out of our love than we have put into it.

I doubt that it will come as a surprise to anyone that those who struggle with selfishness have an especially difficult time embracing the relationship maintenance that is inherent in any long-term love. Because they have such a keen awareness of their own self-interests, selfish men and women have an especially difficult time focusing on the needs and desires of another, even when that other is someone they love. As a result, loving someone who is content in their selfishness will nearly always end up producing a burdensome and deadening love experience.

Conflict and Selfishness

> Self-interest is the enemy of all true affection.
>
> Tacitus

It is a common assertion among marriage experts that conflict between married couples is a given. So if you are looking for someone with whom you are so compatible that conflict will never occur, give up your search right now. Obviously (as we covered in chapter 3), you don't want to ignore blatant areas of difference between you and a partner; such differences will almost certainly lead to irreconcilable conflict later on. So in your search, find someone with whom you have a reasonable level of compatibility, but a search for the harmonious partner is futile.

You see, even if you do find someone with whom you almost never disagree now, you can be certain that conflict will emerge once you are married. There is only one way that two people who love each other can live under the same roof without any conflict, and that is if they are not openly and honestly dealing with the differences in their relationship. So will there be conflict in your marriage? Unequivocally, the answer is yes.

But does this mean that your future marriage happiness is therefore doomed? Not at all. There is something far more important to marital happiness than what a couple disagrees about or even the number of disagreements they have. In fact, many marriage experts contend that these factors are relatively inconsequential compared to the conflict resolution abilities of the couple. In other words, how well a couple is able to work through their disagreements in a healthy and amicable way is far more important to marital happiness than is the inevitable reality of the arguments themselves.[49]

Repeated studies have revealed that when it comes to conflict resolution, one of the key factors in the successful exercise of this skill is what has been termed *perspective taking*.[50] Some people are quite good at perspective taking. They have an ability to put themselves in another person's shoes. They are able to see things from that person's point of view. No matter what the situation, they seem to be able to step out of their own narrow perspective and see things from another angle. It is such people who are particularly adept at resolving conflicts when they emerge.

It is interesting to work with couples who are attempting to resolve areas of conflict within their marriage. Seldom do you hear as the primary complaint from spouses that they don't get their way when disagreements occur. Instead, far more often is the lament that they do not feel heard in the middle of the disagreements. Many married men and women essentially feel as though their point of view, where they're coming from, and what they had to say have not been taken into consideration by their partner. As a result, they feel frustrated, not so much because they haven't gotten their way, but because they haven't been heard.

This brings us (once again) to selfishness. Those men and women who struggle with selfishness are notoriously poor at perspective taking. Because of their inclination to see things from the perspective of what's in it for them, they do not readily take the point of view of a partner, especially when something of self-interest is at stake. Bottom line: a selfish spouse nearly always ends up making conflict resolution a particularly onerous and unfruitful task.

Telltale Signs of Selfishness

> Love is like a tennis match; you'll never win consistently until you learn to serve well.
>
> Dan Herod

As with most character traits, selfishness will play itself out in how one thinks, feels, and acts. As a result, if you are interested in the selfishness level of someone you are dating, then take note of their thoughts, emotions, and behaviors. Below are a few telltale signs of selfishness in each of these three categories. As you take note of these telltale signs, remember that each of us is inclined to be selfish sometimes. That is a given. But what we need to be especially wary of are those *persistent patterns of selfishness* that a person may emit.

How one thinks: If someone consistently agrees with the following statements,[51] then he or she is inclined to be selfish.

- Thinking of yourself first is no sin in this world today.
- The trouble with getting too close to people is that they start making emotional demands on you.

- In striving to reach your full potential, it is sometimes necessary to worry less about other people.
- Having children keeps you from enjoying a lot of self-fulfilling activities.
- In this world, you have to look out for yourself first because nobody else will look out for you.

How one feels: Sometimes emotions are expressed forthrightly. For example, a person might come right out and say, "I am upset" or "I am angry" or "I am frustrated." But most of the time, how one feels is expressed via nonverbal communication. In fact, nonverbal indicators of emotions (tone of voice, body language, eye movements, and vocal intonations) generally provide excellent clues as to what someone is actually feeling.[52] So as you consider the following points, be attentive to those nonverbal responses that a person is *repeatedly and consistently* giving.

- Is this person put out when they have to forego something they would like to do in order to be there for you?
- Does this person respond to minor inconveniences with an overreaction that far outweighs the level of the inconvenience?
- Is this person annoyed when you ask him/her to go out of their way to do something for you?
- Does this person get angry or irritated when things don't go the way they would like them to?
- Is this person confused or annoyed when you suggest that they could be more attentive to your needs and interests?

How one acts: Although many of us are inclined to deny it, what we choose to do is typically a good indicator of where we're really at. As a result, a *persistent pattern* of the following behaviors generally indicates underlying selfish motivations.

- Does this person consistently say that they will do something or be somewhere or get back to you, but something else repeatedly comes up, preventing them from keeping their word?
- Does this person simply go ahead and plan activities with little regard for your schedule or your likes and dislikes?
- Is this person consistently late, sometimes calling at the last minute to let you know they will be late, and at other times simply showing up late, but always assuming that you will be understanding (and then they are put out when you are not)?
- Does this person seldom drop what they are doing (especially if it's something they enjoy) in order to give you the attention or assistance you need?
- Does this person often not respond when you call, even though you know they consistently check every incoming call and text?

Is There Hope?

> Be at war with your vices, at peace with your neighbors, and let every new year find that you are a better person.
>
> Benjamin Franklin

If as you have read this information on selfishness, it has sounded a lot like some individuals you know, then it is important to realize that such people are not currently very good candidates for marriage. Even those who have been able to express the words "I love you," but who are selfish, are not good candidates for marriage. Their level of selfishness is going to be a much better predictor of how many ongoing acts of love they will demonstrate than is the fact that they have uttered these three little words. And as we have seen, such ongoing acts of love are instrumental in whether or not a marriage is going to produce the sort of mutual care, support, appreciation, and respect that every couple hopes for on their wedding day.

Marriages succeed when love works, and making love work depends upon people who work at love. Unfortunately, selfish individuals are not very good at this. And unless you want to become someone's conscience, don't marry a selfish person.

Key No. 8

Love always drowns in a sea of selfishness.

With a selfish partner,

- efforts at we-ness will be stymied;
- bids for connection will be thwarted; and
- attempts at healthy conflict resolution will be frustrated.

Keep your eyes wide open for indications of selfishness—in others *and* in yourself.

But there is hope. As we will see in the next chapter, when people approach their personal shortcomings with an eye for growth, then there is potential for change. And it is in this potential for change that we find a robust hope for a future of lasting love.

The Best Version of You

A Two-Edged Sword

> The quality of a relationship is in direct ratio to the quality of the selves entering into that relationship.
>
> Thomas Howard

One of the hidden benefits of a book like *Intentional Dating* is that its contents wield a two-edged sword. On the one hand, the reader is repeatedly encouraged to make dating a more intentional exercise. This is a reflective process, one in which you become more aware of a variety of traits and behavior patterns that a prospective dating partner may exhibit, and you want to take note of those that have been found to be particularly problematic to the success of long-term love. Obviously, the goal of this reflective process is the development of a more constructive dating process, and ultimately, a more healthy marriage choice. As is true in virtually every other area of life, so too is it true with dating; while we are free to choose, we are seldom free from the consequences of that for which we have chosen.

This is one edge of the sword—becoming more aware of key traits and behavior patterns in others. But there is another edge to this sword. It involves *self*-reflectiveness. Although it is easy to forget, the reality is this. Those very things in others that will inevitably undermine marital success, if they are present in us, will also inevitably undermine marital success. It is not only important to *find someone* who would be a good marriage partner, but it is also important to *be someone* who would be a good marriage partner. Equally important to marrying the right person is to be the right person. When two people marry, and both of them are intent upon being good people, you can expect a wonderful marriage.[53]

Admittedly, we live in a notoriously nonreflective culture. Repeatedly, we have been encouraged to experience life; whether it's been in movies or songs or even in education, we have been told to go out and experience all that life has to offer. But how often does it happen that we are also encouraged to reflect upon that which we have experienced? Not often enough.

And probably nowhere is this truer than in the domain of love. Unfortunately, when it comes to romantic relationships, way too many people have all the reflectiveness of a rock. We go from one love relationship to another, having little to show for it beyond some good times, some bad times, and ultimately, more scar tissue on the heart. Such a nonreflective approach is neither the way to find the love you want (and deserve), nor is it the way to become the loving person upon which a thriving marriage can be built.

Marital Success and Well-Being

If a marriage works, nothing on earth can take its place.

Helen Gahagan Douglas

Marital success is more important than nearly anything else in determining personal well-being. Marital success is far more important to well-being than is money. In fact, those who put a greater emphasis on accumulating money generally end up with a poorer sense of well-being. And this is true even when they are able to accumulate large amounts of it.

Similarly, career success pales by comparison in terms of its impact on personal well-being. For example, in the face of professional setbacks, people's well-being will remain relatively unchanged as long as their marriage is successful. And conversely, if you have an unsuccessful marriage, it doesn't seem to matter how successful you are professionally, your sense of well-being will suffer. The same is true for age, health, education, race, and gender. Bottom line: When it comes to personal well-being, a successful marriage is often the trump card.[54]

So how does one find this pot of gold at the end of the dating rainbow? Over and over again, we have been led to believe that the key to marital success is finding the perfect match. For example, many dating services will promote this point of view: "We will help you find someone who matches your interests, your needs, your traits, and your preferences. We will help you find your perfect match." Does this strike anyone (besides me) as a bit narcissistic? As if matching *my* interests, *my* needs, *my* traits, and *my* preferences is what really matters if *my* marriage is going to work. On top of that, in reality, if what you want is a successful marriage, then you would be wise to give far less attention to matches, and far more attention to qualities.

Don't get me wrong here. It's not as if matching is totally irrelevant. As we discussed in chapter 3, the key to using information about how well you match with someone else is not to find the perfect match, but rather, to avoid those people who are inevitably going to be an imperfect match—those with blatant differences. No matter how strong the feelings of love that you have for someone now, in the long run, blatant differences between you will outweigh strong feelings of love every time, and in the end, those differences will drive a wedge between you.

Far more important than the perfect match for the development of successful long-term love are healthy ways of coping with life circumstances. Similarly, shared priorities are far more important than are shared hobbies. What we value is far more important than what we enjoy. How we handle the unpredictability of life is far more important than what we do for entertainment. In the final analysis, mutual interests are only going to carry a couple so far. Simply put, just because both individuals love to play tennis, enjoy Asian cuisine, are avid snorkelers, enthusiastically follow NASCAR, and can spend hours playing Parcheesi does not in any way suggest that what they have between them is an important basis for love.

In fact, some degree of difference in what couples enjoy can actually have a vitalizing and expanding effect on us as individuals and on a marriage.[55] For example, imagine that one person enjoys musicals more than sports, whereas the other partner appreciates a good football game far more than a good play. It is possible that each person's particular interests can actually end up having an expanding effect on the other. But whether or not this expanding effect can actually emerge from these differences depends on the mentalities with which each individual has entered the marriage. For example, if each person has established we-ness as a priority in the relationship, if each person sees marriage as a partnership between equals, if each person has agreed to value the influence of the other, and if each person is flexible and remains open to new experiences, then the sports' enthusiast can develop an appreciation for the arts, and the theater aficionado can similarly begin to engender a liking for sports.

The Marriage Crucible

> Pain reaches the heart with electrical speed, but truth moves to the heart as slowly as a glacier.
>
> Barbara Kingsolver

Marriage has at times been compared to a crucible. For those unfamiliar with a crucible, let me explain. A crucible is a container that is used for the purification of metal. Essentially, what you do is place the metal in the container, and then as you expose the container to intense heat, the imperfections in the metal come to the surface. Once on the surface, these imperfections can be recognized for what they are—defects—and with some effort, they can be extracted from the molten mass. The end result is a more purified and uncorrupted substance.

Now I realize that most of us are not envisioning marriage as a crucible. After all, marriage is supposed to be a place of acceptance, harmony, and peace, right? Unfortunately, most of us (all of us?) are like metal; we have imperfections. And even if we try not to, we inevitably end up taking these imperfections with us into marriage. And once the appropriate expectations of authentic love begin to be expressed by the one who loves us, then the heat of the marriage crucible begins. How we then decide to respond to this heat will ultimately determine (in the long run) how much acceptance, harmony, and peace we are going to enjoy in the marriage.[56]

Case in point: I grew up in an alcoholic home. If you know anything about alcoholic homes, then you know that they tend to be unreliable, unpredictable, and (to some extent) untrustworthy. Simply put, you can't always count on people to be there for you, even when they say they will. As a result, I learned at a very young age that if I depended on others, then I was setting myself up for disillusionment, disappointment, and hurt.

Now there are many ways in which people who grow up in such an environment can protect themselves from the pain of being let down (again) by the ones they love. For example, they can become people pleasers, trying even harder to win over the consistent love they crave. Or they can become indifferent, essentially saying, "If I just don't care, then I can't be hurt." Or they can rebel, keeping the source of the pain at a distance by rebuffing it in anger. Or they can numb themselves—with alcohol, food, sex, drugs, or entertainment—anything that will keep them from feeling the pain of not being able to count on those who claim to love them.

My response was not any of these. My response was to become highly self-sufficient. Now this was not something that I intentionally decided to do. It was not something that I was consciously aware of, but over time I simply began to rely less and less on others, and more and more on myself. Essentially, if you don't rely on anyone else, then you are less apt to get hurt when they aren't there for you. And this response to my alcoholic home environment worked really well in nearly every area of my life—school, sports, work, male friendships. But then I got married.

I have to confess: when I got married, I thought I was a pretty good catch. But it wasn't long after our wedding day before my wife began to express a desire for more closeness between us. She really did want more interdependence—more of me relying on her and of her being able to rely upon me. She wanted a husband, not a roommate. She wanted two *me*'s actively engaged in the process of becoming a *we*. Let me tell you, our marriage got "hot" in a hurry.

Every Family Is Dysfunctional

> People are like stained glass windows. They sparkle and shine when the sun is out, but when darkness sets in, their true beauty is revealed only if there is light from within.
>
> Elizabeth Kubler-Ross

I have a colleague who has frequently commented that every family is dysfunctional, and in many ways, I have to agree. After all, each of us is human, and each human being is inclined to fail. Even those of us who have the best of intentions and who are diligently conscientious are bound to screw up (at least sometimes). We just are. This is not meant to be an indictment of our families. It is simply an admission of our human condition. There are no perfect human beings, and as a result, there are no perfect parents.

One of our daughters-in-law (a beautiful young woman, both inside and out) was a psychology major here at the University of St. Thomas where I teach. After she and our son were engaged, her parents came to our home for Easter dinner. We were no more than fifteen minutes into the dinner when her mother looked over at me and said, "John, when our daughter took her first course with you, she came home at Thanksgiving and informed us that we had a dysfunctional family." You could have heard a pin drop. One of our other sons (without missing a beat) proceeded to interject: "When I took my first course with my dad, I was certain I came from a dysfunctional family too." What a great comment. Not only did it dispel the tension that was thick in the air, but it also clearly stated a truth that few are willing to recognize.

That having been said, however, we have to admit that some families are more dysfunctional than others. I often think of it as something like psychological, spiritual, relational, and emotional bacteria. Some families parcel out mild forms of these bacteria, whereas others act as a veritable petri dish. But none of us has been spared. Even in the best of situations—for example, those in which parents want to do right for their children, even to the point of participating in parenting workshops—there is potential for mistakes.

For example, when I give parenting talks, I will typically ask parents what it is they want for their children. Almost to a person, parents respond: "I want my children to be happy." My response is inevitably the same. It goes something like this: "If what we want for our children is that they be happy, then we are going to end up making lots of mistakes. Simply put, there are lots of times that we are going to have to make tough decisions, some of which our children are not going to be happy with. Instead, what we should want for our children is that they become contributing members of society; that as a result of their lives, our culture will be healthier; that because they have been alive, our society will be a much better place in which to live."

Furthermore, even if you had the best family on the face of the earth, there is a good chance that somewhere along the road of life you have picked up some bacteria that will end up infecting the vitality of your marriage. As many of us know, this is not a marriage-friendly culture, and therefore, it is easy to acquire traits and behavior patterns that will work against the success of your marriage. In the end, the bottom line is this: the best way to have a good marriage is to be a good person, and none of us is exempt from the need for improvement as a human being.

Finding Your Soul Mate

A person's character is but half-formed 'til after wedlock.

C. Simmons

Young adults were asked what it was that they were looking for in a marriage partner. Almost 95 percent of them stated that, first and foremost, they wanted to find their soul mate. Extensive follow-up interviews revealed that what this meant for the majority of these young adults is that they wanted to find someone who would accept them just the way they are. In other words, their idea of a soul mate is someone with whom you are so compatible that this person will find very little about you that would ever be in need of change.[57]

What an alluring thought. Simply find someone who will accept you just as you are, someone who will not expect significant change, someone with whom you can be happy without either of you doing a whole lot to accommodate the needs and wants of the other. Ah, the soul-mate marriage. It would be virtually effortless. Simply live and let live, with no substantive responsibility or accountability to (or for) anyone. How enticing!

Unfortunately, as enticing as this mentality is, it simply doesn't work—or at least it doesn't work if what you are looking for is a thriving, life-giving marriage. And why would anyone marry if this is not what they're looking for? Essentially, each of us is in need of change—even those of us who are under the impression that we are a pretty good catch.

But some people really don't see it this way. Maybe you've loved someone like this. If you have, then you know exactly what I'm talking about. It's the person who repeatedly asserts in the face of suggestions for change: "You know me. You know that this is the way I am. It's simply part of me—it comes with the package—and if you are going to take me, then you are going to have to accept this with me. If you really love me, then you'll accept me just the way I am."

Beware the person who does not see marriage as an opportunity for change. When someone wants to be loved simply as they are, it does not bode well for the long-term future of their love. Simply put, this way of thinking does not provide a firm foundation upon which stable and satisfying marriages can be built.

In reality, marriage does not work well as a static state, one in which men and women simply remain stationary, unchanged—and unchanging. In reality, none of us comes into marriage fully formed. Whether we are talking about the psychological, the spiritual, the relational, or the emotional, there is a need for ongoing growth and development if we are to become fully functioning adults. The truth is that marriage works best as a formative process, one in which each spouse becomes more fully human, developing more humane sensitivities, as a result of being married. Far more important than finding your soul mate is finding your mate's soul; it is from this that more healthy human beings are able to emerge in the marital union.

We All Have Tails, but We Have to Be Willing to Look for Them

> Self-searching is the means by which we bring new vision, action, and grace to bear upon the dark and negative side of our natures. With it comes the development of that kind of humility that makes it possible for us to receive God's help. We find that bit by bit we can discard the old life—the one that did not work—for a new life that can and does work.
>
> Bill Wilson

Each of us brings some baggage with us into marriage. Admittedly, some of us have more bags packed than do others, but regardless, we all have baggage. And it is this baggage that can take its toll on a marriage.

Remember the crucible—the heat of the marital relationship that brings to the surface our difficult personal traits? That's baggage. For example, I went into my marriage oblivious to the fact that I was so self-sufficient that there was little hope for we-ness to develop between my wife and me. I did not marry with the desire for a growing disconnection from the woman I loved; after all, she was the best thing that had ever happened to me. But in spite of my good intentions, that is exactly what happened. My self-sufficiency made it difficult for us to develop any solid, ongoing foundation for intimacy.

Reasonably enough, my wife began to express a desire for greater closeness in our marriage, and as she did, I found myself confronted by the prospect of change. Now, whenever there is a need for change in a person's life (including my own), I ask what I refer to as the "three questions of change." How these three questions are answered is very important if change is to take place. First, does the person *understand* the nature of the change that is needed? Secondly, is the person *capable* of making that change happen? Thirdly, is the person *willing* to take the steps necessary to bring about the change?[58]

As my wife continued to press for greater closeness in our marriage (and less self-sufficiency from me), I began to ponder the first question. Did I understand what needed to change? Quite honestly, in many ways, I didn't. Self-sufficiency was all I had ever known. As far back as I could remember, I had seldom placed myself in a position of having to depend on anyone, and here I was in a situation (married) where someone (my wife) was asking me to be less self-sufficient—to trust her more, to reveal more of myself to her, to become more interdependent.

It was as if I had a tail. Here was my wife telling me that there was an area of my life that was restricting the love in our marriage, but I couldn't see it. Fortunately, I wanted this love between us to flourish as much as she did. As a result, I was open to checking my rear end in the mirror. After some effort, I found the tail.

This led me to the other questions of change. Question no. 2: Was I *capable* of making the change that was necessary? Question no. 3: Was I *willing* to make the change? For me personally (as well as for many of the people that I have worked with over the years), capability has seldom been the stumbling block to change. Far more often, the key issue preventing a desirable change from taking place has been willingness. As I wrestled with the change that was staring me in the face, I was plagued with one huge question: why change?

Why Change?

> That is what marriage really means: helping one another reach the full status of being persons, responsible and autonomous beings who do not run away from life.
>
> Paul Tournier

As I wrestled with this question, I kept asking myself: "Should I change to please my wife?" After all, she would be so much happier if I would just become less self-sufficient and start connecting more with her, sharing more of what was going on in my life, and depending more on her support and input. Added to this soul-searching was the advice (from a friend years ago at my bachelor's party) that kept reverberating back and forth in my mind: "Always remember, John, a happy wife means a happy life."

I suspect that many of you have been faced with this same sort of decision. Your partner has requested a change, and you have needed to decide whether you should change simply to please that person. Further complicating this type of decision may be the suggestion (sometimes implied, more often overtly stated): "If you really loved me, then you'd change simply because I want you to."

Should you change to please your partner? The answer is: no. Don't change to please your partner. No matter how much you love them, changing to please them won't work. Even if some change does happen, it will be forced, half-hearted, and short-lived. Furthermore, changing to please someone else can often produce anger and resentment. It can even result in score-keeping—"I worked on this change for you, so the least you can do for me is to change this thing about you."

This left me with the question: "Should I change to please myself?" Possibly you have found yourself in this type of situation, one in which somebody you love has requested a change. If you have, then you probably know the answer to this question already. The truth is that I was already quite pleased with the way I was.

Being self-sufficient had served me well throughout my really didn't have any desire to change to please myself. I was already quite happy with who I was.

Then why change? The answer was surprisingly obvious once I began to see it.

I needed to change in order to become a better person. Just because I had experienced a dysfunctional home life did not make it any less true that as human beings, we are meant to have a life of connection, a life of interdependence, a life of relying on others and having them rely on us—in short, a life of love.

Was it easy to come to grips with the fact that I had a tail and that I needed to change? No. And if you know anything about people, then you know that self-sufficiency was not the last tail I had to deal with in my life. In fact, if you know people, then you also know that there are still other tails for me to work through.

Furthermore, if you are aware of these realities, then you also realize that once a person is no longer open to pulling down their pants and checking for tails, then they get stuck in the ruts of life; they stop moving forward; they stop growing. It is then that the human spirit begins to resign itself to the way things are rather than to the way things could be. It is then that the human spirit shrivels up, settling for the unhealthy rather than striving for the healthy, accepting the dysfunctional rather than working for the functional, assenting to the destructive rather than effecting change toward the constructive. And it is then that the baggage we take with us into marriage is allowed to have its eroding effects on the love that was declared so strongly on our wedding day.

Who's to Say?

> He who stops being better stops being good.
>
> Oliver Cromwell

Needless to say, the baggage we take with us into marriage comes in a wide variety of shapes and sizes. Unfortunately, it is not the case that "one size fits all." If it were, then the first few years of marriage would be so much simpler. But in fact, these initial years are anything but simple for a majority of couples.

Imagine how much easier it would be if as we entered marriage, we were informed about those specific personal issues we each possess that are likely to undermine the marital union. Imagine that we were given a heads-up right from the start about those particular personal traits and behavior patterns that we were going to have to deal with if we want our marriage to be a success. Then we would know right from the outset what to anticipate. Then we could be prepared to make the necessary adjustments and changes.

Unfortunately, however, each of our difficult personal traits and problem behaviors vary. The "stuff" that I took with me into marriage is not the same as that of my wife. (Yes, my wife also has had her share of baggage that has been in need of change, but any further details are for her to share.) And the same is true for you. We each have baggage, and far more important than the fact we have it (which is a given) is the mentality with which we face it.

Over the years, as I have encouraged hundreds of men and women to approach their relationship with an eye to becoming a better human being,[59] I have come across quite a few people who have challenged this suggestion. Over and over again, they have asserted: "Who's to say what it means to be a healthy human being? Who's to say what a good person is anyway?" Please be forewarned from the outset. Such a person is not likely to engage in the ongoing discussions about some of the most important issues of life (and effective living) that are so essential to a successful marriage and a thriving family life.

The goal throughout all these discussions in *Intentional Dating* is not to find the perfect person. Having it all together is not a prerequisite for marriage—the training happens on the job.

Besides, there is no such individual. Instead, the goal is to find someone who wants to become the best version of themselves that they can be.

Key No. 9

Find someone—and be someone—who views marriage as an opportunity for change and growth as a human being.

Find someone—and be someone—who wants to become the best version of themselves as a result of being married.

Friendship: The Foundation of Marriage

Love Brings Life and Weeds Choke Off Love

> Isolation breeds deceitfulness; it is easy to fool ourselves into thinking we are mature if there is no one to challenge us. Real maturity shows up in relationships.
>
> Rick Warren

At my son's wedding, I toasted him and his beautiful bride. I held up a rich and robust bottle of wine, and I began to pour it into a wine glass. And as the wine glass became full, the wine began to spill over the sides, and as it did, this was my toast: "May the love you have for one another be as rich and robust as this wine. And may the wine glass of your marriage not be able to hold it all, so that this life-giving love will spill over, bringing life not only to you, but also to those around you—your children, your family members, your friends, your neighbors, your fellow church members, your coworkers, and even the strangers you meet on the street."

Love brings life. Certainly it brings life to the couple who is living it, but it also spills over to those around them. I am sure some of you know exactly what I'm talking about. Simply being with such a couple is vitalizing. We want to talk with them, hang out with them, or even just be at the same party with them—because we walk away enlivened by the experience. Those who are actively living their love bring life.

Isn't this what most of us desire—to love and to be loved in such a way that life flows from that experience? And yet, so often the difficult personal traits and troublesome behavior patterns (the baggage) we each take with us into marriage begin to short-circuit the love that was so fresh and hopeful on the wedding day. It is as if there are weeds slowly and insidiously choking off the love. Just as weeds choke off the growth of healthy plants, shrubs, and flowers in a garden, so too do these "baggage weeds" choke off the growth of healthy love in a relationship.

A few years ago, my wife and I began to cultivate several gardens around our yard. While requiring quite a bit of ongoing care and attention (not unlike a good relationship), these gardens have been a source of considerable enjoyment. I vividly remember when I first started this gardening venture; it was sometimes difficult for me to discern whether what was growing in the ground in front of me was a plant or a weed. Should I let it grow? Or should I pluck it? Similarly, it is sometimes difficult for us to discern whether or not a particular behavior pattern is a weed in our relationship. Is it choking off the love in the relationship or not? The process of learning to discern the weeds from the healthy growth is crucial to the success of every loving relationship, and ultimately, every loving marriage.

The Weeds

> Please teach me to appreciate what I have before time forces me to appreciate what I had.
>
> Susan Lenzkes

Not all weeds are equally unhealthy. For example, in our backyard we have some weeds that typically grow along the fence line. These weeds obviously aren't flowers, but they aren't actively overgrowing everything else in the yard either. As a result, while they aren't the most beautiful things to look at, they also aren't particularly pernicious, so we pretty much just let them grow.

This type of weed is comparable to the quirks and idiosyncrasies that are part of who we are—the loud sneeze in public, the slurping of a favorite drink, the little whistle when we breathe through our nose, the crooked smile, the unconscious cracking of the knuckles—not always pleasant to witness, but not at all pernicious. It is not unusual to find that when love is fresh, we can often overlook these little quirks, and sometimes they are even a source of endearment. But as time wears on, so too can these quirks. What was once just a little idiosyncrasy can begin to take on all the subtlety of fingernails scraping down the black board.

A couple of months ago, I went to coffee with one of my former students, Dave, and his girlfriend, Ashley. Dave had been with lots of women during his university days, but now he had started to get serious about finding someone with whom to spend the rest of his life, so he asked me if I would be willing to give them a "relationship check-up." (Many of my students have affectionately dubbed me the "love doctor.").

Dave and Ashley had been dating for close to two years, and it was obvious that the two of them enjoyed each other's company, that they shared several aspirations and hopes for their lives, and that they cared about each other a lot. But an odd thing seemed to be going on under the table. Every once in a while, I got the impression that Dave was getting kicked in the shins. It wasn't obvious enough for me to say anything at the time, so I dismissed it as one of those errant intuitions that is best left unmentioned.

A few days later, however, I received an e-mail from Dave asking if we could get together to talk. Now you have to understand that Dave is one of those free-spirited, uninhibited, lovable young men who slurps whatever he is drinking, dribbles whatever he is eating, and blurts out whatever comes to mind (only later thinking about the possible implications of what has been said). As it turns out, these quirks did not go unnoticed by Ashley. Dave was indeed getting kicked in the shins under the table.

What to do about these sometimes pesky weeds called quirks? We all have some of them, and even though they are not inherently destructive, they can lead to the slow erosion of love. But the problem is typically not the quirks themselves, but rather, how a partner responds to them.

I have a friend that I have known for years. He lost his wife to breast cancer close to eight years ago. I was talking with him recently in the locker room after working out and he told me: "You know, John, when Mary Jean was alive it was so irritating when she laughed. She had one of those loud, shrill laughs (almost like a tornado siren). Unfortunately, I had a heart the size of a pea when Mary Jean was alive. I would actually get so annoyed when she laughed that I let it get in the way of my love for her. I have to tell you, I would give anything to be able to hear that laugh just one more time."

As for Dave and Ashley, I am still waiting to hear whether Ashley has a heart the size of a pea. If she does, it will be unfortunate, because it will be one more example of a couple who has a lot going for them, but for whom a molehill of quirks has become a mountain of contentiousness. When hearts are small, love will easily be choked off by the insignificant weeds of quirks and idiosyncrasies.

More Weeds

> We have not really budged a step until we take up residence in someone else's point of view.
>
> John Erskine

There is another type of weed that every couple has to work on in their relationship. These weeds are not in and of themselves unhealthy, but how we choose to deal with them can have destructive consequences for the growth of love. These are our personal preferences. We all have them, and since none of us is going to find a personal preference clone, every couple is going to find that they have some differences in what they prefer. For example, one person sleeps with socks on (black, no less), whereas the other wouldn't think of having their feet covered in bed. One likes to spoon while falling off to sleep, whereas the other prefers to lay unentwined. One likes to talk up a storm in the morning, whereas the other prefers quiet time for the first hour after awakening. One likes to clean up after a party before going to bed, whereas the other prefers to take care of the mess in the morning. One likes to...feel free to add your own personal preferences here.

Admittedly, personal preferences can be an annoyance, but they are not inherently destructive; how we deal with them may be, but the fact that we have them is not. If a couple fails to regularly communicate, negotiate, and compromise about their personal preference differences, then these weeds are much more likely to become destructive.[60] If one person insists that their way is absolutely the right way, then these weeds are going to choke off the love in the relationship. If one person refuses to discuss these differences, then what had simply been a difference in preference will become an unhealthy source of antagonism in the relationship. For many of us, working through our personal preference differences is a lot like weeding a garden—not the most pleasant of tasks, but one that nonetheless has to be done (sometimes over and over again).

I would like to offer a rule of thumb that I use when helping couples resolve their personal preference issues. It is a fairly simple principle. It goes like this. If the particular issue you're wrestling with is one where compromise is possible, then pursue a reasonable compromise. For example, one couple I worked with had a huge argument over squeezing the toothpaste—do you always squeeze from the bottom or is it okay to squeeze from the middle? They came up with a compromise—they each use a separate tube of toothpaste.

Sometimes, however, it isn't possible to come up with a solution in which both individuals can get their way. Case in point (using an example from above): one couple enjoyed entertaining, but they had a troubling disagreement about when to clean up. She wanted to clean up before they went to bed, whereas he wanted to take care of things in the morning. Obviously, they couldn't both get their way—unless he simply went to bed and allowed his wife to clean up everything by herself. (Not a good idea!) I encouraged them to talk through this issue with one principle in mind. Who stands to lose the most by not having things done in the way that this individual would prefer? For this particular couple, she found it difficult to sleep if she knew that the house was a mess. He, on the other hand, simply preferred to do it in the morning. They now always make sure that the house is clean before they go to bed.

Destructive Weeds

> I love you not only for what you are, but for what I am when I am with you. I love you, not only for what you have made of yourself, but for what you are making of me. I love you for the part of me that you bring out...I love you because you are helping me to make of the lumber of my

> life not a tavern but a temple; out of the works of my every day, not a reproach but a single song. I love you because you have done more than any creed could have done to make me good.
>
> Roy Croft

Some weeds are truly destructive. One summer, we had what appeared to be a vine growing on a trellis in one of our gardens. Unfortunately, it was a weed, and a highly destructive one at that. Before I realized the damage it was doing, this weed had all but destroyed a flowering vine with which it had become entwined. Fortunately, I noticed the damage it was doing soon enough, so I was able to pluck the weed and nurse the flowering vine back to health.

Remember the self-sufficiency that I took with me into my marriage? This is an example of a destructive weed. Even though I did not initially recognize it as such, it nonetheless started to choke off the love that my wife and I had professed on our wedding day. There are lots of such highly destructive weeds. For example, when we are closed-minded and we regularly lack interest in what our partner has to say, then the growth of love will be thwarted. When we are duplicitous and we lack honesty, then the progress of love will be obstructed. When we are petty and lack generosity, then the maturation of love will be arrested. When we are self-interested and lack a healthy sense of responsibility, then the development of love will be neutralized. When we are impatient and lack self-control, then the unfolding of love will be halted. When we are haughty and we lack appreciation, then the flourishing of love will be abated.

Such traits and behavior patterns that we bring with us into a relationship cannot be accepted as merely quirky weeds. Nor can they be treated as just issues of personal preference. They have to be seen for what they really are—destructive. As with a garden, there is little hope for good things to thrive in a relationship as long as there are such unhealthy traits and behavior patterns that are allowed to grow in the midst of love.

Every couple has to contend with weeds in their relationship; they are simply part of this thing called love. But the goal toward which we are striving cannot be perfection. Anyone who aims for perfection is going to end up with even more weeds than they started with, including anger, disappointment, discouragement, and depression. Simply put, none of us is ever going to be perfectly dependable, or perfectly kind and generous, or perfectly patient. We simply aren't, and to hold out such perfection as the goal is unhealthy, both for the individual who is the perfectionist and for the relationship.

Instead, the goal is improvement. For example, I can tell you that I exude less of that nasty self-sufficiency today than I did thirty years ago. Furthermore, it is my goal that I will have even less of it five years from now. And when I am on my death bed, it is my hope that there won't be much of that unhealthy self-sufficiency left at all. A paraphrased version of one of my favorite quotes captures this well: "Ideals are like stars were to the mariners. They never planned to reach them, but if they ever lost sight of them, they went off course."[61] Even if we intently focus on being dependable or being kind or being patient, we are never going to be able to reach these behaviors completely; after all, we are human. But if we ever lose sight of these ideals, we will go off course.

Talk It Out

> If you don't have time to do it right, when will you have time to do it over?
>
> John Wooden

I am going to make a strong suggestion. It is one that I give to every married couple, every engaged couple, and every couple that is seriously dating. It is arguably the most important piece of advice that I have to give.

Talk! Every week, set aside a chunk of time to do nothing else than talk with each other.

It never ceases to amaze me. No matter whom I ask—my intro-level psychology students, my upper-level psychology majors, engaged couples, or married couples: "What is the number one problem in marriages?" The answer is always the same: "Failure to regularly communicate." We all know what the problem is, and yet, when we look at marriages today, what remains the number one problem? You guessed it—failure to regularly communicate.

Repeated research studies and more marriage therapy cases than we could possibly count have revealed that it is nearly impossible to have a stable and satisfying marriage if a husband and wife do not regularly talk about their life together.[62] If you are currently in a serious dating relationship, I would recommend that you and your partner not wait until you are married to initiate this communication process. Do it now. You need to find out if the two of you can regularly engage in ongoing conversations about those things that are related to the health of your relationship. For anyone who wants a healthy, thriving, and life-giving marriage, an inability to talk things out is a huge warning sign.

Think about it this way. How can a couple ever hope to be able to work through their personal preference issues when they don't have a regular time to talk? Quite honestly, they can't. Nor can they hope to constructively wrestle with their unhealthy traits and behavior patterns if they don't regularly sit down just for the purposes of talking about such things. Obviously, some of these conversations aren't easy. Some of them may even get a little hot (remember the crucible?). But when couples don't directly discuss such issues, seldom does anything change. In addition, the problem behaviors begin to get embedded in the relationship—not unlike the clinging weed that choked off the life in the flowering vine on our trellis.

Why Do So Many Couples Fail to Do It?

> Time is the coin of your life. It is the only coin you have, and only you can determine how it will be spent. Be careful lest you let other people spend it for you.
>
> Carl Sandburg

If talking about your life together is that important (and it is), and if we all know it's that important (and we do), then the logical question is: Why do so many couples fail to do it?

In his insightful little book titled *The Screwtape Letters,* C. S. Lewis describes how a senior devil (Screwtape) instructs a junior devil in the art of leading men and women astray from those things that are most valuable and most important in their lives. One of the first things he mentions is the seductive busyness of life. In the midst of a hectic and frenzied lifestyle around which so much of modern life revolves, those things most precious to us can be eschewed for those things most pressing. In trying to meet all the demands of modern life, it is not unusual to find many couples gradually giving less and less attention to the person (and the relationship) that is most dear. As Screwtape suggests, when people become busy with many things, they are less attentive to those which are most important. We don't even notice that we are beginning to grow apart from the one we love.

The antidote: set aside time every week simply to talk. And if you are anything like most couples, you're going to have to put it into your schedule. Most couples find that they have to literally pull out their calendars every week and find a chunk of time (i.e., at least an hour) where nothing else will happen except conversation. Otherwise, other commitments keep getting in the way, and it simply doesn't happen. And many couples find that in order to accomplish this feat—communicating with no interruptions or distractions for at least an hour—they need to get away from all the commotion and the demands that are so commonly found at home.

Years ago—based on the wise advice of someone we trusted—Kathy and I began to go out once a week simply to talk. This was not a date night. This was not a time when our children were with us. This was not a time to go out and watch a sporting event. This was simply one time per week when there were no anticipated distractions, interruptions, or obligations, a time when we were committed to giving our full and undivided attention to the one we love. I don't think we have missed a week for many years now. It has become a treasured time, a time when we know that we can talk about anything and everything, a time without which many topics would have received nothing more than leftover moments from the busyness of our lives.

Key No. 10

Set aside time every week just to talk about your life together.

Make it happen; carve out the necessary time in your schedule. Otherwise, the busyness of life will end up setting the two of you adrift.

As You Talk: Some Practical Advice

> You can't put yourself in someone's shoes and step on their toes at the same time.
>
> Mark Goulston

When you do sit down to talk about potentially difficult topics, work diligently to avoid the five deadly Ds of conflict resolution: Dictatorial, Demeaning, Disregarding, Disrespectful, and Defensive. People who are dictatorial seldom listen. People who are demeaning seldom appreciate the point of view of another. People who are disregarding seldom give anyone else credit. People who are disrespectful seldom defer to another. People who are defensive seldom change. It is possible to disagree without being disagreeable, but for this to happen, the good of the relationship (*we*) has to take precedence over getting your way (*me*).

As you and your partner work on the various potential weeds in your relationship, there are several points to keep in mind:

- It will often be easier to see someone else's weeds than to see your own.
- All authentic change begins with taking responsibility for your own behavior.
- Focusing on your own responsibility and accountability requires humility and courage.
- Bring to mind people you know who have made significant changes in their lives.
- Don't set out to be perfect.
- Instead, measure success in small steps.
- When you slip up in your efforts to change (that's "when," not "if"), don't fall into self-condemnation.
- When you slip, forgive yourself and recommit yourself to the desired behavior.
- Believe in your own capacity to change.
- Believe in the capacity of your partner to change.

Friends

> Friendship is a strong and habitual inclination in two persons to promote the good and happiness of one another.
>
> Eustace Budgel

Each semester, I express this hope for my students—and I express this same hope for you now. May you marry your friend.

In saying this, part of what I am expressing is a desire that you find someone to marry that you enjoy being with, someone with whom you are able to have fun, someone whose conversation you value, and someone with whom you are able to kick back and simply enjoy life. It is on such a foundation of friendship that successful marriages are begun.

This is what has been referred to as a *friendship of pleasure*. It is good to marry someone with whom you experience this type of friendship. But a quick note of advice here: don't ever take this friendship for granted. It can easily be lost. As the French novelist and playwright Honore de Balzac once wrote: "Marriage must constantly fight against a monster which devours everything: routine."

Every person who has married this type of friend must work to avoid slipping into the mundane trap of habit. "Same-old, same-old" is deadly to a friendship of pleasure. But it doesn't have to be this way. Recent neuroimaging research has revealed that when couples participate together in new and unique experiences, the pleasure centers of the brain come alive with neural activity. Quite literally, the nerve cells in the brain light up, signaling enjoyment. And this is just as true for those couples who have been married for thirty years as it is for young couples who are sharing an experience for the first time.[63] If you are in love with a friend of pleasure, make sure you keep it that way.

But this is only one type of friendship that I hope for you in your marriage. There is another type of friendship upon which every successful marriage is built. This is what I often refer to as a *friendship of utility*. A friend of utility is someone who actively desires to serve. They look for ways in which they can sacrifice their time and energy to meet your needs and the needs of the relationship that you hold in common.

If you want a successful marriage, seek a friend of utility *and* (of course) be a friend of utility. When two friends of utility marry, over and over again they are there for each other. They are actively concerned about their partner's needs as well as the needs of their shared life. Whatever comes, they know they will face it together as a team. It is out of such a mentality that much of our marital satisfaction is able to take root and to grow.

But in addition to friendships of pleasure and friendships of utility, there is another type of friendship upon which thriving marriages are built. It is this third type of friendship that has been the primary topic of the present chapter. This is what has been called a *friendship of virtue*.[64]

A friend of virtue is someone who wants to become a better person. They really do want to change and to grow—to become the best version of themselves that they can. Furthermore, such individuals want to be an impetus of change for others, empowering each individual to become a better person. When you have a friend of virtue as a spouse, then you become actively engaged in the lifelong process of becoming a better human being.

My Best Friend

> You don't marry one person; you marry three—the person you think they are, the person they are, and the person they are becoming as the result of being married to you.
>
> Richard Needham

Kathy and I have been married for over forty years. She is my best friend. When we started out on our marital journey so many years ago, I might have used these "best friend" words, but it would only have been in the sense that she was a friend of pleasure. At that time, I had difficulty putting aside my own needs, wants, and desires in order to be there for her (or for anyone else, for that matter); such is the nature of self-sufficiency. Simply put, I was not a friend of utility. Furthermore, I had a poor sense of what it would mean to become a better human being. In case you haven't picked up on it yet, I was a fairly self-satisfied man at that point in my life. I was definitely not a friend of virtue.

What I have to say next will not come as a surprise to anyone who understands what it takes to nurture a successful marriage. Within three years of saying "I do," the love I had professed so strongly on our wedding day was little more than a faint whisper. If you had asked me at that time, I would likely have told you that divorce was imminent. But somehow, Kathy and I decided that we were going to hunker down, focus on our life together, and give it everything we had to see if we could make it work.

Some of you may be familiar with the following research. A large number of couples were interviewed over an eight-year period. Some of these couples had grown out of love with one another. More specifically, these couples were in the bottom 25 percent of all the couples in terms of their marital satisfaction. They were not happy in their marriages, and nearly all of them were contemplating divorce. Many of these couples, however, decided that instead of divorcing, they would stay together and invest more heavily in their marriage. The findings from this study have surprised nearly everyone, including the investigators. Five years later, a whopping 86 percent of these couples reported that they were now happy in their marriage.[65]

Kathy and I experienced a transformation in our marriage comparable to that of these couples. When people are intent on becoming friends of utility and friends of virtue, as well as friends of pleasure, love will flourish.

Kathy is my best friend, and I can now say that this is true in a much fuller sense than when we were first married. Furthermore, our goal is that this will become even truer the longer we are able to share life together.

Key No. 11

Friends are the ones who bring out the best in us.

Find such a friend to marry—and be such a friend to them.

Marshmallows and Marriage

The Marshmallow Test

> I count him braver who overcomes his desires than him who conquers his enemies; the hardest victory is the victory over self.
>
> Aristotle

It was the spring of 1968. Imagine little four-year-old Tommy sitting in a room at the Bing School at Stanford University. He has just been shown a tray of marshmallows—soft, fluffy morsels of delight. The tray was then set on a table in the front of the room, and Tommy was told by the adult supervisor that he could have two marshmallows once the supervisor returned from running an errand. However, if Tommy wanted one marshmallow now, all he has to do was ring a bell and the supervisor would come back immediately and give him one. Two marshmallows later or one now—that was the challenge presented to little Tommy. Can you imagine his angst?

This scenario with a little four-year old boy captures the classic battle we have all no doubt faced on numerous occasions. Do I delay gratification, or do I give in to what I desire now? Am I going to exert control over my behavior, or do I yield to the present circumstances? Will I persist in my efforts to forego immediate satisfaction, or do I surrender to the appeal of the moment?

In actuality, this scenario was created not just for Tommy, but for 635 children from 1968 to 1974.[66] Of these 635 children, many of them failed to wait until the supervisor returned. For some of these children, they were barely able to wait until he left the room before ringing the bell. Others struggled for a time, only to give up the struggle before the full fifteen minutes was up. And as you might suspect, some of these children simply went ahead and took a marshmallow without even ringing the bell.

For other children, however, there was a conviction that they could do this—that the tantalizing allure of the moment was not as strong as their own ability to resist. They used a variety of methods with which to carry out their determination; for example, some covered their eyes with their hands, others turned around so they wouldn't have to look at the tempting delicacies, others played games or sang songs to distract themselves. But in each case, they believed in their own ability, and they were intent upon successfully exerting their resolve rather than yielding to an easier path that had clearly been laid out before them.

Are You a Two-Marshmallow Person?

> He that would be superior to external influences must first become superior to his own passions.
>
> Samuel Johnson

Years later, these same children were tracked down as adolescents, and the differences between the one-marshmallow and the two-marshmallow children were stark. For example, the two-marshmallow individuals exerted more control over their life circumstances, they were better able to plan and to think ahead, they more successfully adjusted to problems that occurred in their day-to-day lives, they were more adaptable in their relationships, and they performed better academically. One author poignantly described the differences this way: "Those who had resisted temptation at four were now, as adolescents, more socially competent, personally effective, self-assertive, and better able to cope with the frustrations of life. They were less likely to go to pieces, freeze, or regress under stress, or become rattled and disorganized when pressured; they embraced challenges and pursued them instead of giving up even in the face of difficulties; they were self-reliant and confident, trustworthy and dependable; and they took initiative and plunged into projects."[67]

What about you and me? What would we have done if we had found ourselves in little Tommy's shoes? To get some idea of the answer to this question, suppose you were given two alternatives, and you were asked to choose which of the two you agree with more. For example, what if you were asked to choose between these two alternatives: (*a*) "People's misfortunes result from the mistakes they make," or (*b*) "Many of the unhappy things in people's lives are partly due to bad luck?" This is what is called a forced-choice test. You are forced to choose one alternative or the other, even if neither of them seems that appealing. So as you look at these two alternatives, which do you agree with more? (It is understandable if you dislike forced-choice alternatives like these—I dislike them as well—but nonetheless, please select one of the alternatives above.) How about this set of alternatives: (*a*) "In the case of the well-prepared student, there is rarely (if ever) such a thing as an unfair test," or (*b*) "Many times exam questions tend to be so unrelated to course work that studying is really useless." With which one of these are you more in agreement? Let me offer one more: (*a*) "When I make plans, I am almost certain that I can make them work," or (*b*) "It is not always wise to plan too far ahead because many things turn out to be a matter of good or bad fortune anyhow."[68]

As you might suspect, some people tend to agree with the first alternatives in each of these three sets of choices, whereas others tend to select the second alternatives. Those who tend to agree with first alternatives have the qualities of the two-marshmallow children. They generally believe that much of life is controllable, and that through personal effort we can exercise considerable influence over events that affect our lives. In other words, they tend to believe that much of what happens in one's life is more a function of personal dedication and effort than it is luck or good fortune. Furthermore, they are inclined to approach life's difficulties as challenges to be mastered rather than as misfortunes to be avoided.

On the other hand, there are those people who tend to agree with the second alternatives in the examples above. They are more likely to mirror the one-marshmallow children. They are less apt to view themselves as effective agents in bringing about change in their lives. When they set goals for themselves, but then challenges arise, they are more apt to shrink back from those challenges rather than persist through them and figuring out how to overcome the difficulties. In other words, for such individuals, consistently persevering (through thick and thin) with life's challenges and struggles is a dreary prospect that is seldom met with success.

Key No. 12

Find someone—and be someone—who has a strong commitment to being a two-marshmallow person rather than a one-marshmallow person.

Failure to resist the allure of the one marshmallow now in lieu of two marshmallows later will have devastating consequences for marital stability and marital satisfaction.

Why Marshmallows Matter

> Marriage is not a vacation or a picnic. Rather, marriage is a career that demands the very best of both partners. Marriage is a testing ground for one's integrity, courage, and character.
>
> J. Allen Peterson

Two criteria are typically employed to determine marital success. One is the stability of the marital union. In other words, has divorce or separation been allowed to splinter the relationship? For most of us, however, the goal of marriage is not to simply endure it, but to also enjoy it. Therefore, an equally important criterion for success is satisfaction. To what extent are the husband and the wife happy with their life together? Needless to say, marital success in the US is not currently thriving.[69] In fact, if marriage was a business, and we looked at the number of divorces that occur each year as well as the reported lack of satisfaction in the remaining intact marriages, one would be forced to wonder just how this business is surviving.

So why do marriages fail? Why do so many married couples end up so dissatisfied with their partner and with their marriage? Why do so many of them opt to end their marital union? You may be surprised to find out that there are a limited number of reasons why marriages fail. Admittedly, every marriage is unique (because every marriage is made up of unique individuals), but in the end, there are essentially only four reasons why marriages fail.[70] Yes, not thousands (or even hundreds), but four.

You may be wondering what you can do to avoid these four reasons for failing marriages, but please be forewarned. Some of them are inevitable; some are not. Some of them are foreseeable, while others are not. Some are avoidable; some are not. Every couple will experience at least one of them, and some couples will experience all four of them. It is in light of these four reasons why marriages fail that several implications surrounding the character traits of the one-marshmallow person versus the two-marshmallow person take on a unique significance.[71]

Why Marriages Fail, Reason No. 1: Difficult Personal Traits

> A few seem to extract from their childhood the skills and motivation which, as adults, allow them to make extraordinary progress. Some remain trapped by events that occurred long ago.
>
> Clair Carmichael

Suzie and Tony were both in their late twenties when I first met them. Each was happy with their current vocational status, Suzie as the stay-at-home mom of their two small boys and Tony as the manager of a small novelty shop in a busy part of the tourist town where they lived. Their marriage, unfortunately, was a different story. Having met in college and marrying shortly following Suzie's graduation, their marriage had seen its share of struggles. Fortunately, both Suzie and Tony were very open to talking about those first few years of their marriage.

As is true of virtually everyone, both Suzie and Tony had brought some difficult personal traits (baggage) with them into their marriage. Suzie, for example, had grown up in a stable, but conditionally loving, family. The youngest of three children, she had learned at a young age that one of the best ways to obtain affection in her family growing up was through accomplishments. "If I was successful," Suzie stated, "then I was almost certain to receive special attention and appreciation from my parents. For example, when I brought home papers from school that had an A on them, my parents were very proud of me and they told me how much they loved me. But this was something I hardly ever seemed to hear at other times. And then once my name started to appear in the local newspapers (mostly for sports accomplishments, but sometimes for academics), my parents gave me lots of attention and praise. I really did feel loved at those times. But slowly I came to realize that the only times I ever seemed to receive affection was after I had achieved some sort of recognition.

"Well, unfortunately, I took this with me into our marriage. I hate to have to admit it—because it was so unkind and so unloving of me—but during the first couple years of our marriage, I seldom expressed warmth or affection toward Tony unless he was accomplishing something. If business was good at work or if he got a raise, then I would shower him with all sorts of appreciation, warmth, and affection. But at other times (which was most of the time), I was more like a functioning coworker than a loving wife. I hate to even think about it now because I was so unaffectionate toward Tony during those early years."

As Suzie talked, I was struck by the impression that this was not at all the way she was now. She was a very loving individual, especially toward Tony. She repeatedly spoke lovingly about him, and there was a warmth that punctuated the way in which she interacted with him. What I observed from Suzie was not at all how she had described herself. She was anything but cold, removed, and unaffectionate toward Tony.

When I asked about the apparent discrepancy between the impression I had gotten and what Suzie had said, both Tony and Suzie agreed; she had changed. As Suzie explained it, "I went on a retreat one weekend and one of the talks was about love. I came home thinking about what I had heard, and I began to reflect on love—both what I had experienced growing up as well as my expression of love in our marriage. I began to realize more clearly than ever before that while love is unconditional, what I had received at home was not. Nor was my love for Tony. I began to see more clearly than I had ever wanted to that while affection is freely given, what I had received and what I was giving to Tony was anything but. I realized that I had become in my marriage what I so disliked growing up in my family.

"But I was determined to change. I wanted to give Tony the type of affection that rightfully belongs in a marriage. At first it was difficult, but I guess the perseverance I learned in school and in sports paid off. I just kept working at it, noticing all the times when I failed to be warm and loving—and let me tell you, there were a lot of them—and then being more expressive of the love I really do have for Tony. Needless to say, sometimes I was more successful than others, but eventually I began to see a change, and now, I am generally more kind and loving than not." To my delight, Tony wholeheartedly agreed.

Tony's Difficult Personal Traits

Knowledge without courage is sterile.

Baltasar Gracian

Tony had grown up in a verbally and emotionally abusive home. He didn't remember ever being hit, but he did vividly remember the anger that was usually a part of their family interactions. "Both my parents grew up in alcoholic homes," Tony said, "so I guess in some ways they had good reason to be angry. But as I was growing up, it was as if there was a shroud of anger hanging over our family. Everyone was afraid of the next confrontation, and neither my sisters nor I wanted to be the cause of the next outburst. As a result, we learned to be very careful about what we said, and especially anything that might be taken as argumentative.

"The problem is that I have been the same way in our marriage. I am very careful about what I say. Even though I know Suzie is not an angry person, it's as if I'm supersensitive to how she might react to something I say. I don't want anything to turn into an argument. Therefore, I generally just don't say much of anything of substance, which is driving Suzie crazy in our marriage.

"I know that I need to come out of myself more with Suzie. I know that she needs this, and I know that our marriage needs this. In fact, I even know that this would be a good thing for me. But I can't seem to bring myself to do it. Every time I start to talk with Suzie honestly about what I think or to openly express how I feel, and she begins to react in even the slightest way, I clam up and I don't say anything more. I don't want to, but I basically end up stonewalling her. I hate conflict that much. As a result, quite honestly, there's a lot of silence in our marriage."

Tony had some keen insights into the baggage that he had taken with him into his marriage. He could see where it likely had come from in his family of origin. He was able to clearly describe what it looked like in his marriage. He was able to express how difficult it must be for Suzie to have a husband who didn't share his inner world with her. In fact, he even knew that change would be good for Suzie, for their marriage, and even for himself. And yet, his attempts at change had been short-lived at best. It was for this that Suzie and Tony had come to see me. Tony was not able to bring himself to change, and as a result, their marriage was collapsing.

Marshmallows and Change

Life shrinks or expands in proportion to one's courage.

Anais Nin

As Tony and I began working together, it quickly became obvious that he was a bright guy, and his ability to understand his conflict avoidance was impressive. But still, change didn't happen. Somehow, Tony seemed convinced that he was at the mercy of his circumstances. He kept hoping for an easy solution to his marital dilemma. For example, on a couple of occasions he asked me if I could simply wave one of those magic wands that psychologists are supposed to have, and then suddenly the difficult personal traits he had taken with him into his marriage would somehow evaporate and everything would be fine.

Unfortunately, this is not how our personal baggage gets resolved. Far from it. Instead, difficult personal traits get resolved through hard work, and often a good portion of that work entails doing the very thing we think we cannot do. In other words, Tony needed to simply go ahead and engage is some tough discussions with Suzie, even if they ended up producing conflict. But he couldn't, or wouldn't, do it. In the end, this was the stumbling block in Suzie and Tony's marriage. Like the one-marshmallow children, Tony failed to persist in the efforts needed to obtain the prize he really did desire. He repeatedly gave in to his urge to avoid the present struggle of honestly opening up with Suzie, retreating instead into the safe haven of conflict avoidance that had become the easier path for him to take.

In talking with Suzie and Tony, it became obvious that this lack of perseverance was not a trait that had suddenly popped up once they had gotten married. As is almost always the case, such baggage is clearly present long before the nuptial vows are uttered. Whether it was a boss who had it in for Tony, or a teacher who was unfair, or a coach who played favorites, Tony had consistently found someone other than himself to blame for his failed efforts. Furthermore, when challenges emerged, Tony was accustomed to giving up rather than pushing through. For example, even though Tony was a bright young man, he had dropped out of college during a particularly difficult semester his sophomore year (and he never went back). Furthermore, once in the work force, Tony ended up quitting several jobs, in each case when his boss began to have expectations for more productivity and more efficiency on the job.

I wish that I could give you a happy ending for Suzie and Tony's marriage. I wish I could tell you that Tony persistently wrestled with this difficult personal trait (conflict avoidance) that he had taken with him into his marriage. After all, it is a trait that can be changed. But unfortunately, Tony repeatedly concluded that the discomfort he would need to endure in the process of changing was not worth it. He clearly loved Suzie, but he kept hoping that things would simply get better without all the effort and pain that typically comes with change. Unfortunately for Suzie and Tony, change is seldom an effortless and painless experience. They are still married—so they still have stability going for them—but the satisfaction they each experience in their marriage is a far cry from what they had hoped for on their wedding day.

Marshmallows and Difficult Personal Traits

> Truth hurts—not the searching after it, but the running from it.
>
> John Eyberg

It is important to watch for one-marshmallow versus two-marshmallow people when dating. As with Suzie and Tony, the character traits of each are typically out in the open for all to see long before the wedding bells begin to ring. I am often surprised at the number of individuals who overlook the one-marshmallow behavior patterns emitted by their serious dating partner. It would behoove you not to be among them.

Let me quickly add, however, that like most behavior patterns, this one is not impervious to change. For example, not all the one-marshmallow children at age four remained so through adolescence; some of them had emerged in the follow-up studies as personally efficacious, self-assertive, persistent, and unwavering, even in the face of tough situations in their lives. The same is true of us as adults. We are not set like concrete. I have known many young men and women who have struggled with personal resolve in the face of challenging circumstances, only to slowly and painstakingly apply themselves over and over again to the responsibilities set before them each day. When it comes to the qualities of the two-marshmallow people, it is not as if either we've got them or we don't, but rather, they are character traits that are developed. Like muscles, we acquire them as we repeatedly struggle against the weighty responsibilities that life tosses our way. Regardless of how many marshmallows we may have grabbed as a four-year-old (or even as a twenty-five-year-old), it is possible to become a two-marshmallow person. And this is one of the most important lessons that life has to teach us.

So if you are dating someone who has the tendencies of one-marshmallow individuals, talk with them about their apparent lack of follow-through on commitments, their seeming loss of resolve in the face of difficult tasks, and their manifest absence of dedication through thick and thin. See if they are open to change. And if they are, then observe their willingness to put that openness into practice.

In fact, I would be willing to bet that *many of us* are in need of such a discussion. Numerous authors have presented convincing arguments that we are slowly becoming a one-marshmallow culture. There is even empirical evidence that the average young adult today exhibits more one-marshmallow traits than was true of 80 percent of young men and women in the early 1960s.[72] In other words, young men and women today are much less apt to see circumstances in their lives as controllable, they are less apt to believe in their own ability to influence those circumstances, and they are less likely to persevere through thick and thin when difficulties arise. In all likelihood, few of us have been spared, and most of us are in need of ongoing discussion (and renewed resolve) to become more of a two-marshmallow person.

When it comes to the first reason why marriages fail—the difficult personal traits that we take with us into marriage—change typically does not come easily. That's why they've been termed "difficult." They require persistent effort, often over an extended period of time, before noticeable change begins to emerge. As a result, people who are inclined to persist in such effort, even in the face of difficulties, set-backs, and discouragement, are much more apt to experience a stable and satisfying marriage. Such two-marshmallow people are more apt to embrace the challenges of marriage, just as they have embraced the many other challenges that they have faced in their lives.

Why Marriages Fail, Reason No. 2: People Behaving Badly

> Bad marriages don't cause infidelity; infidelity causes bad marriages.
>
> Frank Pittman

There are certain behaviors that simply don't lend themselves to a stable and happy marriage. Simply put, they are bad behaviors. This seems like such a reasonable, obvious, and matter-of-fact statement that when I first started to assert it several years ago, I was unprepared for the comment that I have heard hundreds of times. "Who's to say what a 'bad' behavior is, anyway?" If you are dating someone who is inclined to present this type of argument, beware—eventually you are going to be a victim of their bad behavior.

These bad behaviors that are certain to undermine marital success include the following: incessant gambling, excessive spending, habitual intoxication, frequent self-indulgent behavior, chronic anger problems, compulsive lying, entrenched pornography use, relentless controlling behavior, perpetual procrastination, and a repeated pattern of poor impulse control. If you have been in a serious relationship with someone who has relinquished their struggle with any of these, then I don't have to tell you how destructive these behaviors are. You already know—first hand, up close, and personal.

Don't assume that your love is going to change such behavior. Don't assume that marriage is going to bring about a transformation. Instead, the person wrestling with the bad behavior has to be responsible for any change that is going to take place. It's not that you can't be a source of encouragement and support—because you can—but the trick is to do this in such a way that you are not enabling the person in their bad behavior. Enabling will often seem like a loving thing to do, but enabling is not love.[73]

But none of these marriage-threatening bad behaviors are as common as infidelity. A conservative estimate is that at least 40 percent of married men and 20 percent of married women under the age of forty-five have had an affair. Furthermore, infidelity is frequently cited as the number one reason for divorce.[74]

Like a Plate Full of Marshmallows

> Love is the passionate and abiding desire on the part of two people to produce together an intellectual soil and an emotional climate in which each can flourish, far superior to what each could achieve alone.
>
> Alexander Magoun

There was a time when wearing a wedding ring was a clear indication that you were off limits. This is no longer the case. A while back, I was returning home from giving a talk at a conference, and as I was sitting on the tarmac waiting for the plane to take off, the woman sitting next to me—an attractive woman in her mid-forties—stared at my ring and asked, "Are you *very married*?" I proceeded to explain that I am married to my best friend, that Kathy is the best thing that has ever happened to me, and that we have a great life together. Nevertheless, when we landed, this woman gave me her business card—just in case I ever wanted to reconsider.

In our culture, opportunities for infidelity are going to present themselves. The same is true for gambling, intoxication, drug use, pornography, and a whole host of other issues related to impulse control. Unless you live off on a deserted island somewhere, such opportunities are going to be available—just like the plate of marshmallows that was available to the four-year-olds.

If you are dating someone who struggles with any of these types of behavior, talk with that person. Don't beat around the bush. Be direct. Try to help this individual see and understand the harm they are doing to you, to themselves, and to the relationship. If you are worried about bringing up such a difficult issue, then that is not a good sign. If you are concerned that this person might leave the relationship rather than give up the behavior, then that is a good indication of where you stand in their priorities. If you are afraid of their reaction—feeling as if you are walking on eggshells whenever the topic comes up—then you should take a serious look at the relationship. Walking on eggshells—the feeling that you have to be careful not to bring up a topic that might get the person all riled up—may be a deal breaker. If you find yourself repeatedly walking on eggshells, think seriously about getting out of the relationship.

Once a Cheater, Always a Cheater?

When I have listened to my mistakes, I have grown.

Hugh Prather

Whenever the topic of infidelity comes up in class, I can pretty much count on this question: "If a person has cheated on you once, isn't it true that they will cheat again?" The answer (which applies to many bad behaviors and not just infidelity) is not quite as simple and straightforward as the question itself.

Case in point: Matt and Caroline had met in one of my classes, and they began dating shortly thereafter. They had been dating exclusively for three years when Matt came to see me. They had been talking about getting married (and Matt had even purchased the ring), but something happened recently that threw all their plans up for grabs. Matt had cheated. He was out with friends one night, had too much to drink, and ended up spending the night with a woman both he and Caroline knew from college. Caroline was devastated. Fortunately, so was Matt.

As Matt sat in my office, he poured out his heart. Through a puddle of tears, he blurted out his pain, disappointment, disgust, and regret: "I had never in my life met anyone like Caroline. She is the best thing that ever happened to me. She is the love of my life. Since we've been together, my whole life has just kept getting better. She has made my world come alive in a whole new way. And now I've blown it. I don't know what I was thinking. I am so disappointed in myself. I'm not sure what Caroline has seen in me. I'm afraid I've lost her, and I don't know what to do."

As we talked through the tears, it became very obvious that Matt was personally crushed by what he had done to Caroline. But his devastation was even deeper than this. He was crushed as well simply by the fact that he had done it. This was a very good sign.

The Elephant and the Rider

> Those who do not remember the past are condemned to repeat it.
>
> George Santayana

It turns out that when it comes to dealing with problem behaviors, we have both a rational side and an emotional side. It's not unusual to find that people will sometimes admit in their more rational moments that a particular behavior is unhealthy, but yet their emotional side will not see it for what it really is—disgusting and repugnant. Imagine that you have just changed a baby's diaper. As you look at the feces laying there in the dirty diaper, it would be surprising if you rationally looked at that pile of poop in disgust, but then emotionally wanted to take a bite. But this is exactly what happens with many problem behaviors—we can rationally see the destructiveness of the behavior, but our emotional brain still can't see it for what it really is.

Authors Chip and Dan Heath have described it this way.[75] "Our emotional side is an Elephant and our rational side is its Rider. Perched atop the Elephant, the Rider holds the reins and seems to be the leader. But the Rider's control is precarious because the Rider is so small relative to the Elephant. Anytime the six-ton Elephant and the Rider disagree about which direction to go, the Rider is going to lose. He's completely overmatched." So when wrestling with a problem behavior, one very important key to successful change is getting the Elephant on the same page as the Rider. When the emotional brain supports the rational brain, then there is tremendous energy, power, and drive to reinforce the decisions of the rational brain.

Over the years, I have worked with hundreds of people who have engaged in bad behavior. Some have been able to rationally see their behavior as bad, some have not. If you are currently dating someone who cannot rationally see the destructiveness of their bad behavior, then you should seriously consider getting out of that relationship. Without being able to at least *rationally* see that the behavior is unhealthy, there is very little chance for change.

But the probability of change gets a real boost when an individual not only understands the destructiveness of a behavior rationally, but they are also able to feel it emotionally. Some people I have worked with have wanted to forget what they have done. They want to wipe their infidelity from their memory, pretend their DUI never happened, erase their gambling problems from consciousness, and cancel any recollection of their porn addiction. Then they won't have to deal with the regret that necessarily comes with the memories. But the regret is good. It engages the emotional brain, and that can help enormously to empower a person not to go there again.

Matt and Caroline have just celebrated their eighth wedding anniversary, and they both agree that Matt's moment of indiscretion years ago has been one of the best things that ever happened in their relationship. Even though Matt grabbed a marshmallow when he shouldn't have, he used that bad decision as a jump start for his emotional brain. This has provided an energy and a power from which Matt has been able to make some significant changes in his life. He is now much more careful about who he hangs out with, where he goes, how much he drinks, and how he converses with women other than Caroline. As with all problem behaviors, real change only happens when we initiate drastic alterations in our lifestyle, and this simply won't happen if we merely sit on top of the Elephant holding the reins, but fail to get that big beast of the emotional brain collaborating with the rational brain.

The advice I gave to Matt years ago I still offer to anyone (including myself) who has slipped into bad behavior. Don't ever lose sight of the legitimate regret that is a fitting response to what we have done. It is appropriate that we carry that regret, but not like a backpack full of wet sand that constantly weighs us down and prevents us from moving forward. But rather, we need to use this regret as a way to marshal the forces of the Elephant so they can support the decisions of the Rider. It is good to remember, and not just with the rational brain.

Why Marshmallows Continue to Matter

Why Marriages Fail, Reason No. 3: When Bad Things Happen to Good People

> Even good marriages have recurring seasons, and there can be some hard winters.
>
> Linda and Charlie Bloom

When we love someone, we make promises: "Together, we can handle anything." "No matter what happens, my love for you won't waver." "I will never leave you." And we actually mean it when we say these things. The problem is that life is unpredictable. As much as we would like to control the future and prevent anything disastrous from happening, we can't. We can do our best, but there are no guarantees.

Dan and Teri had just celebrated their first anniversary when Teri was in a car accident that left her paralyzed from the waist down. After several surgeries and months of physical therapy, her condition remained unchanged. Unfortunately, Dan's love for her didn't. He decided to end the marriage. Teri now lives with her parents.

Robert and Hilda, who were high school sweethearts, were married back in the 1950s. Ten months after their wedding day, while on their way to church, an emergency vehicle ran a stop sign and crashed into them broadside. Hilda was thrown from the car, leaving her a quadriplegic, legally blind, and unable to speak. A few years ago, Robert and Hilda celebrated their fiftieth wedding anniversary.

There is no way to be absolutely certain in this life. None of us can know for sure what the future holds. As good as a person may be, there are no guarantees. Sometimes bad things happen, even to good people. It might be a serious accident, the loss of a job, the death of a child, the prolonged illness of a spouse, the problem behaviors of an adolescent, the birth of a handicapped child, or the extended debilitation of a parent, just to name a few. We just don't know what is waiting for us down the road of life. But as Ralph Waldo Emerson once wrote: "What lies behind us and what lies before us are tiny matters compared to what lies within us."

When we marry, none of us is marrying the person who will prevent misfortunes from happening. There is no such person. The goal is to marry someone who will stick with us through thick and thin, someone who will stand with us arm-in-arm against the sometimes vicious waves of life. As many married couples have come to understand, success in marriage is often less dependent upon having everything go right, and more dependent upon how we handle the things that go wrong.

Why Marriages Fail, Reason No. 4: Failure to Keep the Love Alive

The most prevalent failure of love is the failure to express it.

Paul E. Johnson

Maybe you are familiar with SparkNotes (or for older readers, CliffNotes), the series of quick, abbreviated explanations that students have sometimes been known to read in place of much longer original works. What we are going to discuss here as the fourth reason why marriages fail could be referred to as the SparkNotes for keeping love alive. There are hundreds of books out there dispensing advice about how to keep love alive. While there is obviously much to be gained by reading many of these books, what you will find here is a condensed summary of the advice—the SparkNotes, if you will. There are essentially three pieces of advice. The first one is addressed to both men and women, the second is especially applicable to women, and the third is particularly germane to men.

Advice for Both Men and Women: The Nice-to-Nasty Ratio

Kindness is the life's blood, the elixir of marriage. Kindness makes the difference between passion and caring. Kindness is tenderness. Kindness is love, but perhaps greater than love, kindness is goodwill. Kindness says, "I want you to be happy."

Randolph Ray

A young woman (Sophia, age twenty-seven) met a man (Peter, age thirty-two) online, and they each began to pour out their hearts to each other about their troubled marriages. Sophia (whose online name was "Sweetie") told her friends: "It's amazing. We seem to both be stuck in the same kind of miserable marriage. I have found the love of my life. The way this Prince of Joy (Peter's online name) speaks to me, the things he writes, the tenderness in every expression is something I have never had in my marriage." And Peter told his friends: "Sweetie writes such wonderful things to me in our posts. I am so happy to have found a woman who finally understands me."

This went on for weeks. Day after day, Sweetie and Prince of Joy exchanged warm expressions of love. Repeatedly they showered each other with expressions of kindness and thoughtfulness, a far cry from what each of them was apparently experiencing at home. Finally, Sweetie and Prince of Joy decided it was time to meet. They agreed on a coffee shop in the bustling financial district. They would each carry a single red rose so that they could recognize each other. When Sweetie and Prince of Joy saw each other, they were amazed. Neither of them would have guessed that their spouse, the person who was standing there holding a red rose, could have been so kind, attentive, and loving.

John Gottman is one of the foremost love experts in the world, and he has reported that couples who have a 5:1 ratio of positive to negative exchanges have a happy and satisfying marriage. In other words, if for every negative interaction you have with your partner, you have at least five positive interactions, then the probability is very high (94 percent) that you will be able to keep the love alive in your relationship.[76] This is what most of us want, and just think, all we have to do is be more nice than nasty with the person we love. But given the paucity of such ongoing and vibrant love, this is apparently no small feat.

The story about Sweetie and Prince of Joy is true. It was posted on the UK newswire back in September of 2007, and it betrays a telling reality about how we so often end up doing love. We end up treating a mere acquaintance at work (or a seeming stranger on the internet) with greater pleasantness than we treat the one we love. But seldom is the scarcity of such polite expressions of thoughtfulness toward the one we love the result of ignorance. In reality, we understand how to be considerate, attentive, and loving. Nor is the dearth of gentility so often witnessed between partners something that can easily be explained by ineptitude—that we are somehow incapable of consistently treating the one we love with decency and respect. No, the truth is, we understand what it means to be thoughtful and attentive, and we are capable of responding with affection toward the one we love. But are we willing?

There was a movie that was fairly popular a few years ago titled *50 First Dates*. It was one of those cheesy, slightly over-the-top chick flicks that I probably shouldn't have enjoyed. But I did. In the movie, Adam Sandler plays a man who has fallen in love with a young woman (Drew Barrymore) who has been in a car accident. As a result of the accident, the young woman can't remember anything from the previous day. In other words, each day her life begins anew. As a result, she can't remember Adam Sandler, much less how kind, thoughtful, and affectionate he had been the day before.

Adam Sandler faced a dilemma. He loved a woman who could not recall any of his gentle expressions of kindness from the previous day. At the end of the movie, we see the solution. Every day he would once again prove to her how much he loved her. Each day when she would awaken, he was once again warm, kind, thoughtful, and considerate. Each day, throughout the day, he made his affection for her clear through loving words as well as loving actions. He essentially said to her each day: "I love you. I value you in my life. You can trust me with your love. I will not take you for granted. I will not treat your love lightly."

As I walked away from this movie, I found myself thinking about how we so often end up doing love—by not expressing it. Can you imagine how our love would thrive if each day we were intent upon elevating our nice-to-nasty ratio? Can you imagine how we would keep our love alive if each day we were once again determined to be kind, considerate, and thoughtful, persevering in our expressions of affection, over and over again letting the one we love know it?

As you date (and long into your marriage), it would be wise to consider this nice-to-nasty ratio in light of what we know about the traits of two-marshmallow versus one-marshmallow people.

A Piece of Advice for Women: Do Not Be Critical

> Constructive criticism generally isn't.
>
> Linda and Charlie Bloom

Many men marry hoping that their wife won't change a whole lot. After all, he loves her pretty much the way she is—that's why he married her. On the other hand, many women marry hoping that their husband will change. She is hoping that he will take on more responsibility for the life he is leading, for the choices he is making, for the people he is loving, and for the way in which he is loving them. As two marriage authors put it: "More than 80 percent of the time, it's the wife who brings up sticky marital issues, while the husband tries to avoid discussing them. This isn't a symptom of a troubled marriage; it's true of most happy marriages as well."[77]

This all-too-common reality is humorous and not-so-funny, distressing and encouraging, vexing and enlightening, all at the same time, and it creates a dynamic that can have powerful implications for keeping the love alive. Many women facing this reality will drop subtle hints about the changes they are hoping for. I can tell you—subtle hints are not going to work with most of us men. We are not going to get it. In fact, mild suggestions are not typically going to work. With most men, you have to make it clear. But how you decide to make it clear is crucial.

Do not criticize. Criticism is deadly to love. I often tell people that if you want to destroy the love between you and a partner with one fell swoop, then cheat on that person. But if you want to slowly bludgeon to death the love between you, then criticize. The evidence is clear: if you want to keep the love alive, do not be critical.[78]

But please don't interpret this the wrong way. This does not mean that a woman simply has to sit back and say nothing. Not at all. While criticism is deadly to love, there is a huge difference between criticism and a complaint. With a complaint, the person focuses on a specific behavior—for example, "You left your dirty dishes next to the couch last night when you went to bed. I thought we agreed that we wouldn't do that anymore. Can we talk about the agreement we made?" Criticism, on the other hand, departs from the particular behavior and casts dispersions on the person himself: "You left your dirty dishes next to the couch again last night. You are always leaving your stuff around, expecting me to pick up after you. You are such an inconsiderate person. If you think I'm going to be your maid, you've got another thing coming." The specific words you use may vary—we each have our own unique styles for issuing complaints and for leveling criticisms—but the consequences do not.[79]

There is one other very important fact about criticism that needs to be emphasized at this point, and that is this: not all criticism is expressed verbally. In fact, some of the most destructive instances of criticism entail the use of no words at all—for example, the eye roll of disapproval, the glance of contempt, and the sigh of exasperation. Without saying a word, these behaviors signal disappointment, disfavor, and disgust. And in the wake of expressions of criticism (especially if these criticisms comes from someone they love), many men will experience a sense of failure. And for most men, this sense of failure feeds in them a fertile ground of shame.[80]

So the next time you are tempted to be critical, just picture that tray of marshmallows (both verbal and nonverbal)—marshmallows of dissatisfaction, disappointment, or disgust. They are there for the taking. Just reach out and grab whatever is within reach. But remember—the tests we face both reveal *and* develop the character traits of the two-marshmallow versus the one-marshmallow person, and the choices we make do have consequences. Complaints that are stated firmly but lovingly, clearly but calmly, will seldom undermine the love in a relationship, and they may even result in change. But criticism is going to spawn neither the change in someone's behavior nor the love in the relationship that you desire, and in fact, it will likely wound with shame the one you love.

A Piece of Advice for Men: Communicate

> Therapists report that the most common complaint of women in distressed marriages is that their husbands are too withdrawn and don't share openly enough.
>
> Howard Markman

Maybe you have seen the poem that has recently been circulating around the Internet: "Said one young man to his young bride, 'I'm so sad, my dad just died.' 'Let's talk of it,' she softly cried. 'Um, I just did,' the man replied."

Numerous studies (as well as countless therapy sessions) have revealed that the number one reason for marital disaffection is poor communication, most often by the husband.[81] Admittedly, most of us men grow up with limited experience communicating beyond a concrete level of people, places, and things (what has been referred to as report-talk). This is a very factual type of communication. We report, for example, on what has happened—like the young man above who told his wife that his father had died and that he was sad. These are facts. For many men, there just doesn't seem to be a whole lot to communicate beyond this type of information.

But the evidence is extensive and unambiguous; if you want a happy marriage, ongoing conversation beyond a factual level of communication is vital. No couple who desires a happy marriage is going to achieve this invaluable goal if the man fails to regularly communicate information beyond the factual—for example, what he cares about, what motivates him, what he believes in, what makes him tick, and how he is personally impacted by the events of his day. Without this type of communication, couples grow apart. They lose their sense of connection, closeness, and intimacy.

This sort of emphasis on the importance of meaningful, heartfelt communication between a man and the woman he loves is nothing new. In fact, nearly every serious dating couple, every engaged couple, and every married couple is able to spout this truth. And yet, millions of marriages have been sabotaged by a lack of substantive communication. This should rightfully leave us in a quandary. If we have heard that something is true, and we have clear evidence that it's true, and we agree that it's true, but then over and over again it doesn't happen, what's going on?

As we discussed in chapter 8, part of the problem is the busyness of life. But an arguably bigger part of the problem (at least for men) is that communication is difficult. For most of us men, we have had little experience with self-revealing communication prior to our first serious love relationship. For most of us, that is the first time that we have ever had to consider that there might be something more to communication than mere factoids. For example, how many of us men have heard the woman we love say: "We just never communicate?" To which, we scratch our heads, and we say (often just in our own minds rather than aloud): "Never communicate? I don't get it. We just spent the last hour talking. What were we doing if we weren't communicating?" For most of us, it is only after several such experiences that we begin to realize that the woman we love is looking for something deeper. And well she should. Countless studies have conclusively revealed that without this type of deeper communication, marital satisfaction and marital stability will be in serious jeopardy. Marital love is not going to stay alive without it.

This brings us back to the marshmallows. You would never expect to become a skilled guitarist or an effective soccer player or an adept woodworker without embracing the challenges that proficiency demands. Like guitar playing, soccer, and woodworking, communication is also a skill. And as with guitar playing, soccer, and woodworking, we would never expect to become effective without practice. Certainly some knowledge is valuable, but learning by doing is a crucial part of every newly developed skill. As a result, beware the person who is not willing to repeatedly, persistently, and assertively wrestle with the skills necessitated by effective communication. It's not necessary to have already developed these skills—few of us men have—but an unwillingness to sincerely embrace the challenge of improving one's communication skills is a huge red flag that should not be ignored.

[For further knowledge about communication, an effective and straightforward model has been provided in the notes for this chapter at the end of *Intentional Dating*.[82]]

Path of Least Resistance

> There is nothing more lovely in life than the union of two people whose love for one another has grown through the years from the small acorn of passion into a great rooted tree. Surviving all vicissitudes, and rich with its manifold branches, every leaf holding its own significance.
>
> Vita Sackville-West

When I was a kid, there was a small creek in the woods near our home, and one day I decided that I wanted to divert the water in that creek. I had built a rustic club house in some trees a few feet from the creek and I wanted to get the water to flow through the middle of it. I envisioned how cool it would be to have a stream flowing through the middle of my makeshift club house.

For the next several days, I worked at digging out a new ditch for the water—first six inches, then a foot, then two feet deep. When I thought that my ditch was deep enough, I took rocks, dirt, sticks, logs (just about anything I could lift), and I dammed up the creek near the start of my new ditch. Sure enough, the water began to flow right through the middle of my club house. I went home very pleased with my efforts.

But the next day when I went back to the woods to enjoy the fruits of my labor, I was surprised and disappointed to find that the water was no longer flowing through my club house. It had returned to its original creek bed. There it was, following its path of least resistance.

I suspect that many of us have experienced this—not with water in a creek, but with those character traits that are indicative of one-marshmallow versus two-marshmallow people. It is so easy to slip back into a path of least resistance—to quit fighting against our difficult personal traits, to give in to our bad behaviors, to surrender to the tough things that happen in our lives, and to cease our efforts to keep love alive. It is so much harder to be a two-marshmallow person—persistently pursuing that which is good, healthy, and constructive in the long run rather than grabbing what is easy, pleasant, and enjoyable in the short run. When it comes to love, truth has to win out over comfort. Otherwise, we will return to a path of least resistance, and when we do, we will quickly grab all the marshmallows we can get, and love is certain to fail.

Key No. 12: Revisited

Find someone—and be someone—who has a strong commitment to being a two-marshmallow person rather than a one-marshmallow person.

People who are intent on developing the capacity to persevere through thick and thin are better able to

- persist in their efforts to work through difficult personal issues;
- avoid those bad behaviors that are so destructive to marital love;
- remain faithful and steadfast even when bad things befall them;
- maintain a healthy nice-to-nasty ratio;
- resist the temptation to criticize; and
- develop the capacity to communicate with heartfelt meaning.

"How Do I Love Thee? Let Me Count the Ways..."[83]

A Thread

> Most human beings have an almost infinite capacity for taking things for granted.
>
> Aldous Huxley

Have you ever carefully noticed the thread of a garment? Sometimes you might, for example, when a rip has appeared along the seam of a shirt or when a long piece of string has trailed from a pair of pants. But what about in the morning, when you are getting dressed for the day? Do you ever look through the clothes hanging there in your closet and take note of the threads that hold the various garments together? I doubt it.

This is what I experienced as I was doing the background research for my first book, *How to Love Your Wife*. As I read hundreds of articles and books on marital success and marital dissolution, I was like the person looking through their wardrobe at the start of the day. I was focusing on the big picture—the concrete body of information discussed in each of the works I read. Whether the topic was how to resolve conflict in your marriage or how to communicate for greater marital satisfaction or how to avoid the pernicious effects of criticism on marital love, my focus was the same. What does this body of information tell us about how to love the person to whom you've said "I do"?

But slowly my focus began to shift. I don't know exactly when it happened, but gradually, I began to notice a thread, a theme, running through the many research findings and the numerous pieces of advice offered by marriage experts. Maybe it first happened early one morning when I was reading John Gottman's insightful exposition of the keys to a successful marriage (*Seven Principles for Making Marriage Work*). Or maybe the initial realization occurred late one evening as I studied Karen Kayser's careful analysis of marital disaffection (*When Love Dies*). Regardless, my focus slowly shifted to a theme that wove through the numerous admonitions and countless suggestions provided by hundreds of marriage experts.

I began to wonder why I hadn't noticed it before. Over and over again, there it was. When couples had it, love in their marriage flourished. When couples nurtured it, their marriage was an ongoing, life-giving event. But when this thing began to wane, so too did the love in the marriage. When this thing was lacking, so too was the life that the couple once derived from their marital union.

And the more I looked at this thread, the more obvious it became. Couples with it are happy in their marriage; couples without it end up with a growing marital dissatisfaction. Couples with it simply do not divorce; couples without it have stepped out onto the slippery slope of marital demise.

Out of the Blue

> The deepest principle in human nature is the craving to be appreciated.
>
> William James

It was about eight o'clock in the morning when the phone rang in my office. It was a long-time friend of our family. Jeanne graciously asked me if I had time to talk, and when I responded that I had a few minutes to spare, she jumped at the chance to blurt out what was on her mind.

"It's Bob," she said (referring to her husband of twenty years). "He's acting pretty weird, and I'm starting to get a little worried about him." Jeanne had pricked my curiosity, so I asked her if she could elaborate on Bob's "weirdness."

"You know Bob," she said. "In fact, you've known him longer than I have. And you know that he's always had a little edge to him. He's always seemed to be a little negative, sometimes even downright jaded and sarcastic. Well, I had kind of grown used to this over the years. I won't lie to you. His negativity has occasionally slipped into criticism and sometimes it has hurt quite a bit. But I love Bob, and I have told myself over and over again not to take it personally. That it's just the way he is and that he doesn't mean to be hurtful.

"Well, about six months ago, Bob stopped being so negative. Out of the blue, he just stopped. I haven't heard a single complaint come out of his mouth for weeks—no bemoaning his work, no complaining about how expensive everything is, no cynicism about how the world is going to hell in a handbasket. No negativity about me or about our children or their friends. And quite honestly, I think I could have handled all this, but something happened that has pushed me right over the edge of concern.

"You see, not only has the negativity vanished like a ghost in the night, but now Bob has started to express positive things. It seems like every day he's telling me something else that he appreciates about me. One day, it's the outfit that I have on that is so becoming. Another day, it's my smile that he fell in love with years ago. And then it's the meal that I just prepared, or how frugal I am because of the bargain that I just found online, or how much he appreciates the way I put him and our children ahead of myself.

"And I guess I had even been able to take these changes in stride until last night. That's when he held my hand, looked into my eyes, and told me how much he cherishes the fact that I am part of his life. I don't think Bob has said anything like that since our honeymoon.

"John," Jeanne said, "has Bob had a stroke? I know that probably sounds strange and I'm not trying to be overly dramatic, but I remember seeing a movie once where the lead character (I think it was Harrison Ford) gets shot in the head and the damage to his brain changes him from a person who is negative, cold, distant, and uncaring to someone who is positive, warm, tender, and compassionate. Did Bob have a stroke? I can't figure out any other way to explain what's happened. It's so drastic, so sudden, so inexplicable."

I listened intently as Jeanne talked. I too was puzzled. If her account of what was going on with Bob was accurate (and I had no reason to suspect it wasn't), then I had to agree. Bob's behavior was indeed very strange. I reassured Jeanne that I would talk with Bob.

Not a Stroke

> A single event can awaken within us a stranger totally unknown to us.
>
> Antoine de Saint-Expupery

Although I e-mailed Bob shortly after talking with Jeanne, he and I weren't able to schedule breakfast until a couple of weeks later. As I sat in the restaurant waiting for Bob to arrive, I realized that although we had often gotten together to talk in the past, this was the first time we had done so in close to a year. I was sitting there thinking about how quickly time flies at my age when Bob interrupted my ruminations.

As Bob sat down and we began to talk, I was struck by the sorts of things Jeanne had mentioned. Bob really did seem different. I'm not sure I would have immediately been able to put my finger on it if I hadn't talked with Jeanne, but my impression was that he was less bogged down, less thuddy. Instead, he seemed more lighthearted.

We started with the usual discussions about what had been going on at work and what our children had been up to, but that was relatively brief. I am one of those people who are convinced that communication is best when it's direct, when people don't beat around the bush, and when there aren't any hidden agendas, so I launched into why I had e-mailed him to get together.

"Bob, Jeanne called me. She's pretty worried about you." Bob looked over at me with a bewildered gaze. "She's afraid that you've had a stroke or maybe taken a blow to the head that you haven't told her about." By this time Bob was sitting up straight and leaning forward, intently waiting for what I had to say next. I proceeded to tell Bob what had triggered his wife's concerns, and with that, a large smile broke across his face.

With a hint of bemusement, Bob responded, "You know, John, I have changed. A few times Jeanne has insinuated that I'm different, but she hasn't come right out and asked and so I haven't given her any details about what's been going on.

"It all started several months ago. I was at church with my family. The pastor was talking about Ephesians 4:29: 'Let no evil talk come out of your mouths, but only such as is good for edifying, as fits the occasion, that it may impart grace to those who hear.' I started to think about what frequently comes out of my mouth. It was almost like I was watching a video of myself at different times during the day. Let me tell you. It wasn't pretty.

"For the next week or so, I started paying attention to what I had to say and how I said it. To put it mildly, I was disgusted with myself. So often, I would put a cold and skeptical slant on things. I would speak in an irritable and demeaning tone of voice. I was negative in just about everything I had to say. I had always prided myself in being a realist, but what I came to see is that I had become a negative and cynical man.

"Slowly I started to think about giving myself a challenge. Could I do it, I wondered? Could I give up my negative ways of thinking and talking? I thought about it long and hard. You know me. I have always loved a good challenge—as an athlete when I was younger, then as a marine, and now in my job. After thinking about it for a couple weeks, I finally decided to go for it. I was going to quit being so negative and prickly.

"To be real honest, initially it didn't go so well. I am a very determined guy (Jeanne prefers to call me bullheaded), and if I decided not to say anything negative, then I wasn't going to! The problem was that without the negative talk, I didn't have much of anything to say. At times, the silence was very uncomfortable.

"And then I remembered something a sergeant said back in the marines—that very often it is helpful when giving up one behavior if you replace it with something else. That's when I began to look for positive things that I could talk about. That's when I began to tell Jeanne what I appreciated. At first, it was tough. I had spent so many years seeing the negative that it was difficult to spot the positive. But the more I looked for those things that I have every reason to be thankful for, the more of them I noticed. And I was determined to express my appreciation. Apparently it's working."

What a Difference a Change Makes

> *Myth*: It's not good to show too much appreciation. As one man said to me, "If I say thank you all the time to my wife, it would sound phony. By not saying it all the time, it means more to her when I finally do say it." This man was dead wrong. Expressing appreciation is a form of love, and you can never show too much love. If your rare compliments are well received, that doesn't necessarily mean your spouse feels more appreciated. She may simply feel relieved that she isn't as unappreciated as she was beginning to believe.
>
> Paul Coleman

Needless to say, as I walked away from breakfast that morning, I was glad to know that Jeanne's fears were not a reality. Bob had not had a stroke. But I have to admit that there was something else that gave me even more enjoyment. It was Bob himself. Certainly he was more upbeat and positive about life in general, but what especially struck me was how he talked about Jeanne. He had a renewed fondness for her. He was clearly pleased that she was in his life.

Bob had changed, and in many ways what he had done was very basic and straightforward. He stopped being so negative, irritable, and sarcastic. He started focusing on the many things in his life for which he has every reason to be pleased. He began to notice more and more of the things about Jeanne, their marriage, and their family that he appreciated, and he found ways to express those things.

In fact, Bob himself described his process of change in very straightforward terms. He referred to it as his four-step process. "Step 1, I was determined to be less negative and to be more positive with Jeanne and the kids. Step 2, I acted on my determination. I actually spoke in ways that were more positive and more encouraging. Step 3, I listened to myself and I took careful note of my successes—and my failures. Step 4, I repeated steps 1, 2, and 3." Bob was quick to add: "I guess in some ways, I'm still using this four-step process, but I think I'm beginning to see more successes than failures."

Months later, Bob was still unable to explain just why he had made the changes he did, except to say: "I knew that it was the right thing to do. I knew that at one time my fondness for Jeanne was deep and heartfelt, and I also knew that deep down, that fondness for her was still alive. I had buried it under a mound of negativity and cynicism, but I knew it was still alive. All I had to do was dig it out from under the rubble."

Key No. 13

> Find someone that you are fond of, someone that you admire, someone that you regard with warmth, affection, and respect.
>
> Find someone who is fond of you, someone that admires you, someone that regards you with warmth, affection, and respect.

The reasons Bob gave for his stark behavior changes were straightforward and uncomplicated. So were the effects of those changes. The affection between Bob and Jeanne began to grow. More and more, he enjoyed their time together. He looked forward to coming home to Jeanne and the children. They began to go on dates reminiscent of their early years together. He began to appreciate Jeanne as much as he did when she first began to light up his life years before. As Bob told me, "This is what I thought marriage was going to be all along. I never would have dreamed that the changes I made would have had such a huge impact on my marriage—and I love it!"

What about Jeanne?

> Appreciation unlocks the fullness of life. It turns what we have into enough, and more. It turns denial into acceptance, chaos into order, confusion into clarity. It can turn a meal into a feast, a house into a home, a stranger into a friend. Gratitude makes sense of our past, brings peace for today, and creates a vision for tomorrow.
>
> Melody Beattie

As for Jeanne, she was overjoyed by the changes in her husband. More and more, she looked forward to the time they had together, and she found herself buoyed by his upbeat, encouraging, and optimistic disposition. At times she wondered whether there wasn't something deeper behind Bob's decision to change, but she never pushed him for more of an explanation. She was simply grateful for the changes. It was very life-giving to be told consistently that she was appreciated by the man she loved.

As time passed (and Bob's changed behavior didn't), Jeanne began to notice that things in her life didn't seem to bother her so much anymore. The challenges of work didn't weigh on her as much, the occasional struggles of (and with) her children didn't pull her down as badly as they used to, and the blue moods that used to sweep over her (seemingly out of nowhere) virtually disappeared. And as Jeanne began to understand the origins of Bob's behavior changes, she had a newfound appreciation for his "bullheadedness"; having a strong will can be quite an asset when it's pointed in the right direction.

I doubt that any of us would be surprised to find out that Bob and Jeanne's marriage is thriving. Little had they suspected years ago on their wedding day that they would have grown so far apart, but negativity, pessimism, and lack of appreciation will do that to a marriage every time. These behaviors will slowly drain the life and energy out of any relationship.

But Bob had stumbled on a powerful antidote for what ailed his languishing marriage, and he embraced it wholeheartedly. His persistent positive disposition cast a pleasant hue throughout their home. His expressed fondness for Jeanne restored a fresh love and energy to their marriage. His obvious appreciation for her created an inviting and energizing atmosphere for their life together.

Months later, Jeanne talked with me about some of her reflections on Bob's far-reaching behavior changes. "In many ways," Jeanne said, "I think I had been struggling with depression. These blue moods would just sweep over me, and I would find myself in a funk, sometimes for days. And I have to admit, they were getting more frequent. I even considered going to a doctor. But since Bob has changed, those blue moods are becoming just a vague memory."

In a moment of deep insight, Jeanne had this to add: "Do you have any idea what it's like to be so busy, to work so hard, *so that you will be appreciated*? It's exhausting. I hadn't realized I was doing it, but I can now see that many times I worked really hard just in order to be appreciated. But now, since it is expressed so clearly, I know that Bob is thankful that I'm in his life, and this knowledge has been rejuvenating. It is so freeing to do all that I do *because I am appreciated*, not *so that I will be appreciated*. I am still just as busy as I was before (maybe even more so), but I hardly ever notice it now.

"But you know, as much as I love the fresh energy I have, and as much as I am really glad that I no longer get swept away by those bouts of sadness, I think the thing I am enjoying the most is that my appreciation for Bob has gotten a real shot in the arm. I'm starting to recapture that fondness I had for him when we were first married. He really is a great guy, and I love him. And it is so good to be in love again."

Don't Wait

> If you can't be happy without your partner, you won't be happy together.
>
> Linda and Charlie Bloom

Be positive. Be accepting. Be optimistic. Develop a capacity for fondness.

I am surprised by the number of young people I talk with each semester who have plans to become positive, pleasant, and good-natured—once they get married. The sentiments of a young woman I talked with last week are indicative of this perspective. She said, "Once I find Mr. Right, then I'll become that person who will be a good partner. I'll be warm and energetic. After all, I'll be with Mr. Right. I'll be easy to live with and fun to come home to. Once I find the right person, then everything will fall into place."

Don't wait. Start now. Don't make finding Mr. Right (or Ms. Right) a prerequisite for becoming a positive, optimistic, and pleasant person. The longer you wait, the more difficult it's going to be. Besides, finding that person is going to be much more difficult without these traits than with them; one of the best ways to find a good person is to be a good person.

It is amazing the number of marriages that begin their slow descent into the marital trash heap simply because someone has ceased to be an enjoyable companion. People don't just fall out of love. If love dwindles, it's because people have ceased doing the little things, the everyday positive expressions of fondness, respect, and appreciation that say in a hundred ways: "I'm a very lucky person to have you in my life."

Practice now—with friends, with roommates, with family members, with the person at the checkout counter. Develop the skill of exchanging a pleasant comment with those you come across. Make it a habit to smile at those with whom you interact.

Exchange a laugh with at least one person each day. Express compassion for those who need it. Share joy with those who are experiencing it. Give at least one compliment per day. Become a person who is capable of ongoing warm, friendly, and positive exchanges. Become a person capable of sincere fondness. Without these qualities, love is doomed.

Key No. 14

Fondness, admiration, appreciation—these qualities are at the heart of every successful marriage.[84]

Find someone—and be someone—who desires to nurture these qualities.

Gratitude

Maximizers and Satisficers

> Nothing is enough to the person for whom enough is too little.
>
> Epicurus

Imagine that you are out shopping for a pair of jeans. Are you the type of person who finds a really good pair of jeans (for example, great fit, appealing style, and good price), but you feel that you have to check out a few more stores before you decide to buy—just in case the perfect pair of jeans is four stores down the street? Or are you more the type of person who has found a really good pair of jeans (great fit, appealing style, and good price), so you buy them—why look further when you've already found a really good pair of jeans?

What about television viewing? Some people may be watching a program that they really are enjoying, but they continually feel the need to click through the other options that might be available. For other individuals, however, once they find an enjoyable show, they are quite content to simply leave that program on without repeatedly checking for other alternatives.

These are examples of what Barry Schwartz has referred to as *maximizers* versus *satisficers*. Maximizers are people who want to make the optimal decision. Whether it's a clothing purchase, a video rental, or selecting a gift for a friend, maximizers tend to keep checking options, even if they've already found what would be a very good choice. Satisficers, on the other hand, tend to be satisfied once certain standards have been met. This doesn't mean that satisficers settle for mediocrity—their criteria can be quite high, but as soon as their standards have been met, they tend to make a decision and take action.

Research discussed by Schwartz[85] (in his best-selling book titled *The Paradox of Choice*) has revealed that maximizers

- take longer to decide on a purchase;
- engage in more product comparisons;
- tend to feel less positive about their purchasing decisions; and
- spend more time thinking about alternatives that they may have passed up.

You might be wondering: what does the purchasing behavior of maximizers versus satisficers have to tell us about love and marriage?

Maximizing, Satisficing, and Love

> He is a wise man who does not grieve for the things which he has not, but rejoices for those which he has.
>
> Epictetus

In some of the research we have been conducting at the University of St. Thomas, we have been studying the connection between maximizers versus satisficers and several aspects of loving relationships. For example, when it comes to the prospect of marriage, maximizers are far more doubtful, uncertain, and ambivalent than satisficers.[86] Remember the extended product comparisons and the delay of purchasing decisions for maximizers? These same characteristics appear to spill over into commitments to marriage. If you have hopes for a commitment, but you are dating a maximizer, it is important to realize that your partner may end up shopping for a very long time before deciding to buy.

In another series of studies, we have been investigating maximizers versus satisficers and their openness to the three primary components of love: intimacy, passion, and commitment. When in a serious relationship (whether dating or married), maximizers score lower on all three. They score lower on intimacy (i.e., how much they are willing to communicate with their partner), they score lower on passion (i.e., how strong are their feelings of affection for their partner), and they score lower on commitment (i.e., how much they perceive a future together with their partner).[87] In other words, even though maximizers and satisficers may both say, "I love you," maximizers are inclined to experience less intimacy, less passion, and less commitment in their love relationships. Just as maximizers tend to be less positive about their decisions in the world of product purchasing, so too in the world of love.

What about giving their attention to people other than their current partner? For example, suppose people are asked the following question: "I flirt with people of the opposite sex without mentioning that I am in a serious relationship." Are maximizers more apt to agree with this statement than are satisficers? The answer is yes. Just as with shopping, maximizers tend to be attentive to alternatives that they may have passed up. Furthermore, maximizers in a serious relationship are more apt to cheat on their partner. Like the shopper, they are apparently still looking for that perfect pair of jeans. Finally, maximizers have revealed a much more positive attitude toward divorce. An easier return policy makes perfect sense for someone who is often plagued by buyer's regret.[88]

[For anyone interested in responding to the complete Maximizer Scale (and scoring your responses), please see the notes for this chapter at the end of *Intentional Dating*.[89]]

Cure for the Maximizer

> Happiness is not having what you want, but wanting what you have.
>
> Rabbi H. Schachtel

Suppose you have come to realize that you (or someone you love) is probably a maximizer. Is there any hope? Yes, definitely. But the antidote is not easy. The first thing you will need to do is the very thing you don't want to do. If you are shopping and you find that really good pair of jeans, buy them. Resist the urge to shop further. If you are watching a television program that you are enjoying, stick with that program. Withstand the impulse to channel surf. For a maximizer, this is a very difficult thing to do.

Furthermore, once you have made your choice and are sticking with it, work on your thinking. It won't do much good to make a decision and then spend the next several hours (or the next several days) ruminating about all the what-ifs. Essentially, maximizers have a difficult time being grateful for what they have.[90] This makes perfect sense. When you are continually thinking that something better might be out there somewhere, it is difficult to be satisfied with what you have. Therefore, if you are a maximizer, it is important to work at developing a way of thinking that will allow you to be grateful for that which you do have rather than regretting that which you may not.

An excellent example of such thinking can be found in many of the world's proverbs. They frequently encourage (often in brief sound bites) gratitude for what we already possess. For example, take the following proverbs:[91] "A lame foot is better than none" or "The smallest fish is better than an empty dish" or "Better a crust than no bread at all" or "I complained that I had no shoes until I met a man who had no feet." People who are able to embrace such proverbs tend to experience gratitude for what they have, and they spend far less time lamenting over that which they don't. As the Turkish proverb says, "For the grateful, the gnats make music; for the ungrateful, harps and flutes make only noise." It is vital to understand that gratitude enriches, whereas ingratitude diminishes. If you ultimately want a happy marriage, develop a capacity to be grateful. Love in the hands of the grateful thrives. Love in the hands of the thankless shrivels up.

A Little Experiment

> In writing his autobiography, G. K. Chesterton wanted to find one sentence that described what life was all about. In that one sentence, he said, "The critical thing is whether we take life for granted or whether we take it with gratitude."
>
> Christopher Peterson and Martin E. P. Seligman

Are you open to a little experiment?[92] It would go something like this. Each of us would be instructed to journal every night for a month. We would simply be asked to sit down for five or ten minutes each night before going to bed and write about our day. Simple enough, right?

Here's the catch: half of us would be instructed to journal only about those things in our day that had not turned out as we might have liked—events that were disappointing, frustrating, or aggravating. We would focus only on those things that had happened at work, on the road, with friends, or with our partner that were negative, unpleasant, or upsetting. We would focus our attention only on the negative, and we would write as much detail as possible about how each of these events had been a source of discouragement.

For the other half of the people in our little experiment, they would be asked to write each night about events from their day that had been positive, pleasant, and encouraging. Every night for a month they would focus only on the positive. Reflecting on their day, they would write only about that for which they were grateful, expressing in writing what it was they appreciated from their day—at work, while driving, with friends, and with their partner.

After a month, which group do you suspect will experience a greater increase in gratitude? If you guessed the latter group, you are correct. In numerous studies, it has been found that one of the best ways to develop a greater capacity for optimism, hopefulness, and positivity is to sow mental seeds of gratitude. It's true; ultimately, we reap what we sow, and those who sow seeds of gratitude end up reaping an attitude of gratitude, and the benefits of this gratitude are far-reaching.

One of the benefits of gratitude can be found in close relationships. Grateful individuals have a greater appreciation for the important people in their lives, and the more things about these people they grow to appreciate, the more grateful for them they become. And as this gratitude increases, so too does the individual's understanding, compassion, congeniality, and helpfulness. But the benefits of gratitude don't stop there. Research has also revealed that grateful people lead longer, happier, healthier, friendlier, more loving, better adjusted, more moral, more productive, and more successful lives.

So if you desire a happy relationship, don't be a person who focuses on what you've missed out on, what you've been deprived of, or what you lack in your life; whatever you focus on expands in your consciousness. Such thinking will only lead to greater negativity and greater ingratitude, and without gratitude, the heart begins to dull. As you (and possibly the person you love) consider a life of continued affection for one another, strive for gratitude. It will sustain you (and your love for one another) in unique and life-giving ways as you travel together on this journey called life.

The Bruise

> Bitterness imprisons life; love releases it. Bitterness paralyzes life; love empowers it. Bitterness sours life; love sweetens it. Bitterness sickens life; love heals it. Bitterness blinds life; love anoints it.
>
> Harry Emerson Fosdick

Imagine that someone begins to pound on your thigh with their fist. They do this not once, but a hundred times. And then imagine that as you are restrained, the pounding continues until you have a massive black bruise covering your whole thigh. Needless to say, that entire region of your leg would be extremely sensitive to the touch, and if you were then to get hit, you would probably either lash out or you would create distance—the classic fight or flight response. If you had such a bruise, this would be an understandable response, even if someone hit you accidentally.

Some of us have experienced just such a bruise in our lives (but not one that is physical), and that bruise can have devastating effects on our capacity for ongoing gratitude and affection. Consider, for example, Don and his fiancée, Carrie. I had gotten to know Don quite well as a student in three of my classes, so when he asked if I could get together with him and Carrie over coffee, I was not at all surprised.

Don and Carrie wanted to talk about a struggle they were having in their relationship. Carrie described it this way: "Don seems so sensitive to anything I say that might suggest he's not perfect. I'm starting to feel as if I can't even make a simple suggestion without him getting hurt. Sometimes he gets angry with me, and at other times he just gets quiet and distant. Eventually we end up talking about it, and Don is always apologetic, but it keeps happening, and I don't know what to do.

"Let me give you an example. Just last night, we were talking about wedding plans, and I gently suggested to Don that it might be good if he is clean-shaven for the wedding. It's not that I don't like him with his beard, because I do, but I just think the wedding pictures would be better without one. Well, Don got upset and then he clammed up for the rest of the night. He apologized this morning, but this seems to be happening so often that it's beginning to have a deadening effect on our affection for each other."

I looked at Don to get his take on what Carrie had just said. He agreed, apparently as much at a loss as was Carrie. But as the conversation continued, Don began to talk about his relationship with his dad: "My father can be pretty demanding. As I was growing up, it never seemed like I could do anything that pleased him. It felt like he was always criticizing me. Whether it was work around the house, or a sport that I was playing, or my grades at school, he was never satisfied. I remember once when I was maybe twelve or thirteen, I had been especially careful mowing the lawn (which was one of my jobs). I had mowed the grass in very straight rows, just like my father wanted it, and I trimmed the whole yard very thoroughly. It looked really sharp, and I couldn't wait for my dad to come home to see it. When he got out of the car that evening, all he said was, 'You missed a spot over there. Can't you do anything right?' I was devastated. And this event seemed to epitomize my entire life growing up. No matter what I did, it seemed that all I got from my father was disappointment and criticism."

Don had a bruise. It was as if he had been pounded on so many times by his father that now he was hypersensitive to any suggestion of failure. Unfortunately, his bruise had begun to spill over into his relationship with Carrie. Bruises almost always do. The hypersensitivity that bruises create has a unique capacity to impede the free flow of gratitude and affection on which love feeds.

Attributions

> People's thoughts about their partners shape the quality of relationships.
>
> Anita Vangelisti

Every couple who has dated longer than a few months has had to wrestle with attributions.[93] These are the explanations we conjure up in an effort to explain someone else's behavior. For example, suppose that you have been preoccupied lately, and there have even been a few times when you've been downright distant. How does your partner explain this behavior? To what does he or she attribute emotional distance?

Sometimes the attributions we make are external; for example, "She's under a lot of stress at work right now" or "She hasn't been sleeping very well lately, so she's probably really tired" or "She's really been having a tough time with her roommates lately, so no wonder she's distracted." Such attributions seldom disrupt the relationship, and in fact, they may even serve to strengthen it if a partner sees this as an opportunity for understanding and support. Sometimes, however, the attributions are more internal; for example, "She is such a moody person" or "She is only nice when she wants something from me" or "She's clearly not into me as much as I'm into her. I wonder if there's somebody else." Understandably, such internal attributions will typically undermine the closeness in the relationship.

As long as attributions emerge from a reasoned and logical point of view, they are typically of an external variety.

Unfortunately, however, not all attributions are reasoned, and when an area of hypersensitivity has been struck, they seldom are. When a person's bruise has been hit (even inadvertently), the resulting attributions are seldom charitable and loving. For example, Don rationally knew that Carrie loved him, and yet, almost against his own logical reasoning, when he felt devalued and hurt, he reacted to Carrie in a way that failed to demonstrate the love he actually had for her. It was as if an emotional reaction was set in motion by the feelings of hurt, and these feelings then ended up overpowering his expressions of love for Carrie.

If you (or someone you love) struggle with areas of hypersensitivity, here are some suggestions. First, be reflective. Work at understanding the nature of the sensitivity; for example, when does it typically occur? What sets it off? What do the customary reactions look like? While some people have a need to know where the bruise actually came from in the first place, this is not nearly as important for change as is the knowledge of how the bruise works now. Getting a handle on the past is seldom as important as understanding the present. Reflect on the process. Develop an understanding of how the bruise operates. Very little change will happen without this understanding.

Secondly, don't date someone who is likely to strike a bruise over and over again. I am often surprised by the number of people who are hypersensitive to criticism who end up dating critical individuals, or the number of people who have trust issues who date those who are untrustworthy, or the number of people who feel inadequate who date people who take them for granted. Fortunately for Don, Carrie was not a critical or demeaning individual.

Thirdly, work at becoming more objective. When an area of sensitivity has been struck, an emotional reaction (rather than a rational one) typically ensues. When this happens, subjectivity quickly rushes in to replace objectivity. If reason doesn't fight to override this emotional reaction, then the negative feelings are going to be free to run amuck. When faced with such a situation, it is essential that we learn to tell ourselves the truth. For example, over time, Don learned to tell himself the truth about Carrie (and about himself)—she was not intentionally putting him down; she wasn't thinking less of him; she was not being mean or nasty; she is entitled to share her opinions; she really does love him; he really is hypersensitive; he really does overreact sometimes; he really does have a bruise.

I am happy to report that Don and Carrie are doing well. They recently celebrated their tenth anniversary. The last time I talked with Don, he told me that he still overreacts sometimes; emotional habits don't die easily. But he quickly added that his bouts of hypersensitivity are getting rarer all the time, and when they do happen, both he and Carrie have learned to recover quickly. It was enjoyable to talk with Don. It was obvious how fond he is of Carrie and how grateful he is that she is a part of his life. As Don and I finished talking, I found myself reflecting on their sincere love for each other. It so easily could have been snuffed out by Don's hypersensitivity, but fortunately, he has been willing to do the work necessary to overcome his bruise.

Unforgiveness

> A good marriage is simply the union of two awfully good forgivers.
>
> Carole Mayhall

Have you even wondered how to catch a monkey? One method (which a friend of mine from South Africa told me is still used today) is to take small pieces of fruit (for example, bananas), and place them inside a jar that has a small opening at the top. The monkey comes along and sticks its hand inside the jar, grabbing the fruit. As long as the monkey continues to hold onto the fruit, its fist is too large to fit through the opening at the top of the jar.

All the monkey has to do in order to get free is let go of the fruit, but it continues to hold on; it's caught.

This is what unforgiveness is like. We have been offended, and with that offense come hurt, anger, and resentment. We hold on to the offense—along with the emotional reactions that have come with it—and once in the grip of these emotional reactions, we become embittered, hardened, and distant. Even if the offending party is a partner whom we love, once we have been offended, we can lose our positive, tender, grateful, and warmhearted responsiveness to that person. All we have to do is let go of the hurt, anger, and resentment, and then we will be free. But we refuse to let go; we're caught.

The reality of all loving relationships is that they are comprised of human beings, and as a result, there will be offenses committed. It is inevitable. Hopefully these offenses will more often be unintended than intentional, but nonetheless, they will happen (even for the most loving of people). And when they happen, the capacity to forgive—to let go—is vital to the life of the relationship. A wealth of recent research evidence has revealed that the capacity to forgive is one of the essential ingredients in successful marriages.[94]

Are you a forgiving person? And if you are dating someone, how about that individual?[95] Do either of you hold grudges? Are you slow to let people off the hook? Is it difficult for you to let go of an offense and to move forward in a relationship? Do you have long-standing bitterness and resentment toward family members or friends? If this sounds like you (or someone you love), then know that this will be a barrier to your ongoing experience of gratitude and affection.

Furthermore, when someone has a bruise, they are much more likely to take offense, even when an actual injustice has not been committed. Take, for example, Don and Carrie? Carrie was not even able to make a mild suggestion without Don feeling offended, getting angry, and creating distance in the relationship.

So I have to ask: Are you easily offended? How about the person you are dating? Does that individual take offense quickly? If the answer is yes, then you are even more vulnerable to the devastating effects of unforgiveness in your capacity to maintain an ongoing experience of love.

Learning to be a more forgiving person is a process, as is learning to be less hypersensitive. For many of us, these transformational learning processes are not easy, but if we want a love that will survive the test of time, then the effort will be well worth it. These character traits will pay huge dividends as we strive to develop and maintain a lasting love. Without them, fondness will repeatedly be thwarted, gratitude will routinely be neutralized, and affection will regularly be blocked. But with them, fondness will be preserved, gratitude will be sustained, and affection will be safeguarded.

If You Are Grateful for Someone, Let Them Know

> Feeling gratitude and not expressing it is like wrapping a present and then not giving it.
>
> William Arthur Ward

In the Psychology of Marriage and Family course I teach, there is one assignment given each semester that for many students is more difficult than anything else I assign—more difficult than the research papers, more difficult than the exams, and more difficult than the reflection papers. For this assignment, each student is instructed to think of someone in their life who is very important to them—someone for whom they are grateful—and they have the task of telling that person just how thankful they are for them and why.

When the assignment is first given, the discomfort in the classroom is palpable. Some people want to know if this really is a course requirement, and if so, how much it will count toward their final grade. To such questions, I explain that the completion of the assignment *will* be counted toward their final grade, but that the true test of their mastery of the assignment will come later—when they are actually living out a lifelong love. Other students express concern about completing this assignment face-to-face; are they allowed to do it via e-mail or a text? The answer is no. Still, other students want to know what this has to do with learning about marriage and family. To this type of question, I calmly try to describe the importance of telling someone how much they are valued; without this, fondness is sure to shrivel up.

Needless to say, we live in a culture where such gestures of personal gratitude are rare. We seldom give such verbal honoring, and we seldom receive them. In fact, negative humor is far more common than are expressions of gratitude. For example, I was recently standing near a group of young married couples, and I overheard one of the men say about his wife: "She asked for something shiny that will go from zero to two hundred in seconds, so I bought her a scale." He was clearly trying to be funny, and it worked—everyone in the group was yucking it up—but as I glanced over at this man's wife, through the feigned smile were the signs of a deep wound. Obviously, negative humor can be very entertaining, but it typically occurs at the expense of someone else, and very often that someone else is someone we love. As a result, I regularly encourage couples to eliminate negative humor from their relationship. The laughs we might generate are never worth the potential damage to the one we love.

The assignment given in class—to go and tell someone how grateful you are that they are a part of your life—is the antithesis of negative humor. Each semester, students complete the assignment, and each semester, most do it with considerable struggle. It's not easy to sincerely and forthrightly express to someone how much they mean to us and why we are grateful that they are in our lives. This is simply not something with which many of us have much practice. It's rare to grow up doing it, and it's seldom modeled for us by anyone in our environment. And yet, it is a vital piece in the puzzle of love. Without this piece, the picture is incomplete. Without it, the type of ongoing affection most of us hope for will come up short.

Honoring

> Gratitude is a sure index of spiritual health.
>
> Maurice Dametz

Years ago, my wife and I began to talk about the fact that neither of us was very proficient at this skill of expressing gratitude. Neither of us had much experience with this type of behavior while growing up (and admittedly, I was particularly deficient in my capacity to express fondness and gratitude). After some discussion, we decided it would be good to give everyone in the family practice with this skill. Therefore, we introduced something new into the family as our children were growing up. We decided that whenever we celebrated someone's birthday, we would take a little time for everyone in the family to honor the birthday person. The only rules were the following: (*a*) everyone had to say something, (*b*) what was said had to be positive, and (*c*) what was said had to be true.

When we first started doing this, it was sometimes awkward and stilted. Frequently, both the person doing the honoring as well as the one on the receiving end felt twinges of discomfort. Oftentimes what was said was trite. For example, I vividly remember one of our sons telling his older brother that he really appreciated him for his big muscles. But we persisted; after all, this is a skill, and a skill can be learned.

I am happy to tell you that over the years these birthday celebrations have been a rich source of expressed gratitude. Certainly these times are uniquely special for the person whose birthday we are celebrating; knowing that the most important people in your life love you and are grateful for you is a very life-giving experience. But equally special is the learned skill of letting those you love know it. This is a very doable skill, and it is one that is necessary if we are ever going to experience the life-long love that we hope for. Practice this skill. Find people in your life that are special to you, and let them know just how grateful you are for them. Don't let awkwardness or discomfort hold you back. The benefits you will reap are enormous.

Key No. 15

Find someone—and be someone—who wants to be a satisficer rather than a maximizer.

Find someone—and be someone—who cultivates an attitude of gratitude.

Find someone—and be someone—who is intent on

- overcoming personal areas of bruise;
- maintaining positive attributions; and
- being a person of forgiveness.

Find someone—and be someone—who expresses gratitude to those they love.

The Love Bank

Marital Success: It Comes Down to Love

> Keep love in your heart. A life without it is like a sunless garden when the flowers are dead. The consciousness of loving and being loved brings a warmth and richness to life that nothing else can bring.
>
> Oscar Wilde

Willard Harley[96] has given us a wonderful analogy of the Love Bank. You and the one you love (either now or in the future) have a Love Bank. You have countless opportunities every day to make love deposits. And as with any bank, you can also make withdrawals. Obviously, the goal is to have a flourishing account where the love deposits far outweigh the love withdrawals. Unfortunately, when we look at the current landscape of fractured marriages, it appears that there may be too many overdrawn accounts.

Needless to say, there are many challenges that married couples have to face. For example, nearly every couple comes into marriage with different likes and dislikes, with different ways of doing things, with different expectations, and with different areas of personal struggle. Furthermore, many of us have to learn how to communicate, how to negotiate and compromise, how to solve problems, and how to resolve conflicts. But these are all surmountable challenges, learnable skills, and doable tasks—as long as we keep the Love Bank full. I am convinced that no single area of marriage has as great an impact as this. As long as the Love Bank is full, virtually everything life has to throw at us is manageable. But when the Love Bank is depleted, even the littlest things begin to take on an exaggerated importance.

That's what *Intentional Dating* is all about—the Love Bank. We have been talking about how to find someone—and how to be someone—who is going to make more love deposits than love withdrawals. Such people

- want authentic love, not simply an in-love experience;
- treat others with kindness and respect;
- work at cultivating an interesting and stimulating life;
- are true to their word;
- seek a vibrant, ongoing connection with God;
- view dating as more than simply an opportunity to be entertained together;
- establish appropriate sexual boundaries;
- approach dating with the intention of finding a marriage partner;
- give their attention to genuinely good-hearted people;
- strive to squelch their inclinations toward selfishness;
- approach marriage as an opportunity to become a better human being;
- want to be a friend of pleasure, a friend of utility, and a friend of virtue;
- have a strong commitment to persevering through thick and thin;
- nurture fondness and appreciation;

- cultivate an attitude of gratitude;
- want to be forgiving; and
- are grateful and express it regularly.

The challenge of rich married love is not an easy one; it requires that you maintain a sizable positive balance in your Love Bank. This is not an easy accomplishment, but it is one that is well worth the effort. Couples who live this type of love are enlivened by the experience. They are able to face the daily responsibilities of living more bravely, more energetically, and more fruitfully. They have life to give, and they give it freely. It is my hope that you (and the one you love) desire this type of marriage, and I hope that *Intentional Dating* has helped you understand how this type of love can be accomplished. It is an incredibly life-giving love, and our world is badly in need of more of it.

Notes

Introduction: The Adventure of a Lifetime

1. Cox and Demmitt (2014) reported that when a large cross-section of people were asked what they would wish for if they were given one wish, the vast majority expressed a desire for meaningful love.
2. In their book titled *The Case for Marriage,* Waite and Gallagher (2000) have presented a challenging review of over 150 empirical studies pointing to these many benefits afforded married couples. More recently, Parker-Pope (2010) has summarized numerous research articles indicating the advantages of married life.

This Thing Called Love

3. Whitehead and Popenoe (2001) reported that a large majority (86 percent) of the 1,003 young adults sampled (ages 20–29) agreed that marriage is hard work. These findings were reported as part of *The State of Our Unions,* an annual report published by the National Marriage Project (now housed at the University of Virginia). The National Marriage

Project was initiated in response to the growing dearth of information on the state of marriage and family life in the United States. Popenoe and Defoe-Whitehead (1999) began the inaugural edition of *The State of Our Unions* with the following statement: "Amid reports of America's improving social health, we hear little about the state of marriage. How is marriage faring in American society today? It is becoming stronger or weaker? Sicker or healthier? Better or worse? Answers to these questions from official sources have been hard to come by. The federal government issues thousands of reports on nearly every dimension of American life, from what we eat to how many hours we commute each day. But it provides no annual index or report on the state of marriage. Indeed, the National Center for Health Statistics, the federal agency responsible for collecting marriage and divorce data from the states, recently scaled back this activity. As a consequence, this important data source has deteriorated. The National Marriage Project seeks to fill in this missing feature in our portraits of the nation's social health with *The State of Our Unions*" (p. 3). I am reminded of the admonition offered by Stephen Covey (noted author of *The 7 Habits of Highly Effective People*): "I am convinced that if we as a society work diligently in every other area of life and neglect the family, it would be analogous to straightening deck chairs on the Titanic."

4. Michele Weiner-Davis is a renowned marriage therapist and author. Among her many works are the following books: *Divorce Busting: A Step-by-Step Approach to Making Your Marriage Loving Again,* and *The Sex-Starved Marriage: A Couple's Guide to Boosting Their Marriage Libido.*
5. Gary Chapman (2004) began his best-selling book, *The Five Love Languages*, with a poignant distinction between love and the in-love experience.

6. In an article titled "What Is This Thing Called Love?: Defining the Love that Supports Marriage and Family," Noller (1996) discussed the multi-faceted nature of love. She went on to provide empirical evidence for the type of love that (*a*) provides high levels of relationship satisfaction, (*b*) is most supportive to the well-being of family members, and (*c*) offers the greatest stability to family relationships. This type of love that Noller described is the antithesis of the in-love experience, a conclusion that has been confirmed by other authors as well (e.g., Chapman, 2004; Rempel & Burris, 2005; Smith, Nunley, & Martin, 2013; Sophia, Tavares, Berti, Pereira, Lorena, Mello, Gorenstein, & Zilberman, 2009; Sussman, 2012; Weiss & Schneider, 2006). For a summary description of the various ways in which love has been defined, and which of these types of love are associated with marital success, see DeGenova, Stinnett, and Stinnett (2011).
7. Patz (2002) described the findings from intensive interviews with 168 newly married couples [conducted by Huston, Surra, Fitzgerald, and Cate (1981)]. It might surprise you to find that those couples for whom romantic love was the strongest were especially vulnerable to divorce. In the words of Patz, "Believe it or not, marriages that start out with less 'Hollywood romance' usually have more promising futures" (p. 60).
8. Numerous researchers have reported that declines in relationship satisfaction over the first few years of marriage are not unusual; furthermore, couples' openness to embracing the new challenges of being married are important to long-term marital success (e.g., Bradbury & Karney, 2004; Clements, Stanley, & Markman, 2004; Creasey & Jarvis, 2009; Huston, Caughlin, Houts, Smith, & George, 2001; Kurdek, 1999; Scott, Rhoades, Stanley, Allen, & Markman, 2013).
9. Numerous authors have expressed the need for ongoing romantic expressions of affection within a marriage (e.g.,

Caughlin & Huston, 2006; Debrot, Schoebi, Perrez, & Horn, 2013; Gottman, Gottman, & DeClaire, 2006; Haltzman, 2013; McCarthy & McCarthy, 2003). In fact, a case can be made that no marriage will be able to thrive without them (Harley, 2008).

10. Mike Adams is the author of *Natural Health Solutions* (2006).

The Romantic Love Complex

11. The article by Goode ("The Theoretical Importance of Love") appeared in the *American Sociological Review* in 1959.
12. The interested reader can refer to Lantz, Britton, Schmitt, and Snyder (1968) for more information on the derivation of the four components of the Romantic Love Complex.
13. In a Fox News Opinion Dynamics Poll conducted in February of 2005, a sample of 900 men and women were polled about love at first sight. Almost two-thirds (64 percent) stated that they believe in love at first sight, and 58 percent said that they had experienced it.
14. For recent reviews of findings about twenty-first century dating derived from dating service experience, see Conkle (2010) and Finkel, Eastwick, Karney, Reis, and Sprecher (2012).
15. Love (2001) described the workings of dopamine, norepinephrine, and phenylethylamine to produce the blinding infatuation experience. In describing the cross-cultural evidence deriving from the extant infatuation research, she concluded: "When you look at societies with the least stable marriages and the highest divorce rates, they are the ones that use infatuation as the sole or major criterion for marriage" (p. 37).
16. Jankowiak and Fischer (1998) found evidence in 166 different cultures for beliefs about love that were consistent with a love-is-blind mentality. However, in most of these cultures

(the U.S. excluded), such thinking was viewed as a force to be wrestled with, rather than as a normative experience to which we should ascent when in love. When it comes to this component of the Romantic Love Complex, Van Epp (2008) may have said it most succinctly when he stated: "Healthy love is not blind" (p. 27).

17. Knox and Schacht (2008) reported on a study of the love attitudes of 1,027 undergraduates. When asked about love and life's struggles, "More than 80 percent (81.7 percent) agreed that 'deep love will get a couple through any difficulty or difference'" (p. 73).
18. The findings reported here—that over 50 percent of college students say they would divorce if the passion died in their marriage—are based upon the article titled "The Association Between Romantic Love and Marriage" (Simpson, Campbell, & Berscheid, 1986). For a more recent discussion of these findings, see Hatfield and Rapson (2008).
19. Hendrick and Hendrick (2006) summarized the findings from several studies of couples' marital happiness. They reported that passionate love is consistently the strongest predictor of marital satisfaction across a wide range of ages.
20. Several studies have revealed that having multiple serial dating partners is associated with less marital satisfaction and greater marital dissolution (e.g., Meier, 2003; Paik, 2011; Rector, Johnson, Noyes, & Martin, 2003).
21. Kephart (1967) asked college students the following question: "If a man or woman had all the qualities you desired in a mate, would you marry this person if you were not in love with him or her?" Seventy-six percent of the women and 35 percent of the men stated that they would marry that person. Asking the same question almost twenty years later, Simpson, Campbell, and Berscheid (1986) found that 20 percent of women and 14 percent of men agreed with this statement. A recent sampling of over 150 students at the University of

St. Thomas revealed that only 10 percent of the women and men agreed.

22. Therapists Barry and Emily McCarthy (2004) summarized the research on romantic love this way: "Our culture's glorification of romantic love...subverts marriage...[Here is a] self-defeating promise of romantic love: If you love the spouse, everything will flow. This seductive cultural myth is reinforced by songs, movies, and novels. In truth, being swept away by romantic love...predicts marital problems and sexual dysfunctions" (pp. 76–77). [Please note: the term "jerkette" was coined by Van Epp (2007).]

Eyes Wide Open

23. In summarizing the research on dating dos and don'ts, Olson, DeFrain, and Skogrand (2011) emphasized the need to observe how dating partners treat other people. They advised that you should "look for someone who is respectful and kind to everyone" (p. 287).
24. It is not surprising to find that numerous studies have revealed that spouses' negativity toward one another is associated with increased marital conflict, decreased marital satisfaction, increased marital distress, increased marital disengagement, and decreased marital stability (e.g., Antonucci, Birditt, & Ajrouch, 2013; Caughlin, Huston, & Houts, 2000; Epstein & Baucom, 2002; Ganiban, Spotts, Lichtenstein, Khera, Reiss, & Neiderhiser, 2007; Johnson, Cohan, Davila, Lawrence, Rogge, Karney, Sullivan, & Bradbury, 2005; Knoke, Burau, & Roehrle, 2010; Roberts, 2000).
25. The power of reinforcement to maintain and strengthen behaviors is a long-established principle in psychology (and in life). Those behaviors that are rewarded (for example, by our loving attention) tend to be repeated. Furthermore, the more they are rewarded, the more frequent they become. This is

true for both healthy and unhealthy behaviors. Unfortunately, people can inadvertently reinforce unhealthy behaviors through their attention and affection (Myers, 2013).

26. There is a growing body of empirical evidence that relationship success is tied to people's self-control and their capacity for taking personal responsibility for their actions (e.g., Baumeister & Tierney, 2011; Finkel & Campbell, 2001; Tangney, Baumeister, & Boone, 2004; Vaillant, 2012; Vohs, Finkenauer, & Baumeister, 2011). In her summary review of what it takes to have a successful marriage, DeGenova (2008) emphasized that one of the keys is the capacity for ongoing personal accountability.
27. For the astute reader, you will notice that family of origin issues come up frequently in *Intentional Dating.* It is not uncommon to find that experiences from our family of origin influence our romantic love reactions, interactions, and decisions. For those individuals who are interested in learning more about family of origin issues, the following books provide valuable and accessible information: *Family Ties that Bind* by Ronald Richardson, *Cutting Loose* by Howard Halpern, *Healing the Shame that Binds You* by John Bradshaw, and *Getting the Love You Want* by Harvey Hendrix.
28. Trust has repeatedly been discussed as one of the keys to a successful marriage; for just a small sampling of the resources emphasizing the importance of trust to relationship success, the interested reader can see: Buyukcan-Tetik, Finkenauer, Kuppens, and Vohs (2013), Gottman, Gottman, and DeClaire (2006), Goulston and Goldberg (2002), Laaser (2008), and Miller and Perlman (2009). Bottom line: if you want a successful marriage, find someone who is trustworthy.
29. For those readers who would like to better understand how one's family of origin can influence mate selections, and how to keep from making the same mistakes over and over again, please see (for example) the following books: Gunther

(2010), Hemfelt, Minirth, and Meier (2003), Norwood (2008), Piorowski (2008), and Van Epp (2008).

30. The evidence is clear; when people marry someone who is blatantly different from them in such areas as temperament, values, beliefs, religiosity, or life goals, seldom is the union satisfying and stable. Olson, DeFrain, and Skogrand (2011) have provided a thorough review of the literature in this area.
31. For excellent reviews of the literature on the importance of religious involvement in the success of marriage, see Mahoney, Pargament, Tarakeshwar, and Swank (2008), Paloutzian and Park (2013), Spilka, Hood, Hunsberger, and Gorsuch (2009), and Welch (2010).

What Is Dating for, Anyway?

32. There is arguably no greater predictor of long-term relationship success than the capacity to enjoy one another's company (see Gottman & Silver, 1999, 2012; Harrar & DeMaria, 2007; Howell & Jones, 2010).
33. Several researchers have found that intense romantic sexual relationships result in an increased activity in those parts of the brain associated with reward experiences and addictive behaviors, with a corresponding decreased activity in those brain regions associated with critical thought and rational judgment (e.g., Aron, Fisher, Mashek, Strong, Li, & Brown, 2005; Bartels & Zeki, 2000; Curtis, Liu, Aragona, & Wang, 2006; Hatfield & Rapson, 2008). The title of Parker-Pope's (2007) *Wall Street Journal* article discussing this line of research is telling: "Is It Love or Mental Illness?: They're Closer Than You Think."
34. For those readers interested in the empirical evidence linking pre-marital sexual behaviors to an increased risk of divorce, please see: Heaton (2002), Laumann, Gagnon, Michael, and

Michaels (1994), Rector, Johnson, Noyes, and Martin (2003), Teachman (2003), and White, Cleland, and Carael (2000).

35. A *Washington Post* article by David Brown in 2011 (titled "A Sweeping Survey of Americans' Sexual Behavior") reported the following: "The latest round of the National Survey of Family Growth found that among fifteen to twenty-four-year-olds, 29 percent of females and 27 percent of males reported no sexual contact with another person ever."
36. In 2003, the Institute for American Values published a book titled *Hardwired to Connect.* Those readers interested in evidence that the desire to love and to be loved is in our nature would do well to read this well-documented work. More recently, several authors have developed this idea in popularized books. For example, David Walsh (in a book for parents titled *No: Why Kids of All Ages Need to Hear It and Ways Parents Can Say It*) had this to say: "We are hardwired to connect to other people. In fact, a lack of connection can cause a 'failure to thrive,' which can be fatal for babies and young children" (p. 51). Similarly, in a book for young adults (*Unhooked*), Laura Sessions Strepp said: "The need to be connected intimately to others is as central to our well-being as food and shelter. If we don't get it right, we're probably not going to get anything else in life right either" (p. 8). As a third example, Brene Brown (*Daring Greatly*) stated: "Love and belonging are irreducible needs of all men, women, and children. We're hardwired for connection—it's what gives purpose and meaning to our lives. The absence of love, belonging, and connection always leads to suffering" (pp. 10–11).
37. Fowers (2000) reported that 96 percent of Americans have a strong desire to marry at some point in their lives, "a figure that has not changed over the past thirty years" (p. 31). A recent Gallup Poll has confirmed that 95 percent of Americans still express a desire to marry.

38. The age at which people are marrying for the first time has been steadily increasing for the past 60 years. In the mid-1950s, the median age for marriage was twenty-two for men and twenty for women. Now the median ages are approximately twenty-nine and twenty-seve for men and women, respectively (Cox & Demmitt, 2014)).
39. Heaton (2002) reported that the inverse relationship between age at first marriage and marital success held true for marriages that took place prior to the age of twenty-one. He reported that after twenty-one, increasing age is not predictive of more successful marriages. More recently, Glenn, Uecker, and Love (2010) reported that the greatest likelihood of successful marriages was found among those who married at approximately ages 22–29. These findings (which were based upon a sample of over 20,000 couples) were obtained for both college graduates as well as for those with less education.

We Give Power to Those We Love

40. Reviews of the research (e.g., Cole, 2005; Knapp, 2006) have revealed that deception is a common occurrence in dating relationships. Furthermore, in the world of online dating, Conkle (2010) has stated that "lying is ubiquitous" (p. 14).
41. The statements cited in *Intentional Dating* (i.e., "I demand the best because I am worth it" and "If I were on the Titanic, I would deserve to be on the first lifeboat") came from the questionnaire most commonly used to measure narcissism, the Narcissistic Personality Inventory (Raskin & Terry, 1988).
42. Twenge (2011), Twenge and Foster (2010), and Twenge, Konrath, Foster, Campbell, and Bushman (2008) have provided careful analyses of data from the past twenty-five years indicating that narcissism is on the rise among young men and women.

43. For more information on what makes some people more susceptible to the narcissist's allure (e.g., in love with being in love, good-heartedness, and low self-esteem), see Brown (2010) and Wilson (2009).
44. For excellent descriptions of narcissistic behavior patterns and reviews of the narcissism research, see Campbell (2005) and Twenge and Campbell (2009).

Narcissism's First Cousin

45. As with narcissism, there are numerous indications that selfishness is also on the increase in Western cultures (see Campbell & Miller, 2011; Twenge, 2006).
46. Several authors (e.g., Bahr & Bahr, 2001; Impett & Gordon, 2008; Stanley, 2005; Stanley, Whitton, Sadberry, Clements, & Markman, 2006) have provided arguments and evidence for the value of sacrifice and the deleterious consequences of selfishness within the context of marriage. As DeGenova (2008) succinctly stated: "It is not surprising, therefore, that the most successful marriages are based on a spirit of mutual helpfulness, with each partner unselfishly attending to the needs of the other" (p. 186).
47. Numerous authors have concluded that those couples who develop a clear bond of we-ness in their marriage have the greatest levels of marital stability and satisfaction (e.g., Buehlman, Gottman, & Katz, 1992; Dalton, 2007; Gottman & DeClaire, 2002; Gottman & Silver, 2012; Goulston & Goldberg, 2002; Reid, Dalton, Laderoute, Doell, & Nguyen, 2006; Seider, Hirschberger, Nelson, & Levenson, 2009).
48. Relationship maintenance is necessary if marital stability and satisfaction are to be sustained. As Canary, Stafford, and Semic (2002) stated: "Spouses need to engage continually in maintenance activities...The efficacy of most maintenance strategies depends on their continued use" (p. 403). Numerous

researchers have discussed selfishness-related variables as an encumbrance to ongoing relationship maintenance (e.g., Baker, McNulty, Overall, Lambert, & Fincham, 2013; Canary & Dainton, 2006; Ogolsky & Bowers, 2013; Stafford & Canary, 2006; Weigel & Ballard-Reisch, 2008).

49. Most marriage therapists agree that conflict in marriage should be expected. As Howell and Jones (2010) put it, "Some couples say that they never fight. While that sounds wonderful, it may be a danger sign, as couples who never have disagreements are more likely to divorce than couples who do…Disagreements between people in a close relationship are inevitable" (p. 88). Eshleman (2003) explained it this way: "Conflict is not viewed as bad or disruptive of social systems and human interactions; instead, conflict is viewed as an assumed and expected part of all systems and interactions… Because conflict is quite natural and to be expected, the issue is not how to avoid conflict but how to manage and / or resolve it. In so doing, the conflict, rather than being disruptive or negative, may force change and perhaps make relationships stronger and more meaningful than they were before" (p. 19). In the words of Markman, Stanley, and Blumberg (1994): "It's not how much you love one another, how good your sex life is, or what problems you have with money that best predicts the future quality of marriage… The best predictor of marital success is the way you handle conflicts and disagreements" (p. 6).
50. Stosny (2006) summarized a wealth of research when he stated: "Your marriage cannot be successful unless you strive to see your partner's perspective. You must learn to understand it and to value it" (p. 233). Consistent with this assertion, Van Epp (2007) contends that the inability to see things from another's point of view is one of the most important criteria in deciding who not to marry. Furthermore, research has revealed that one of the things that interferes with perspective taking

is selfishness (e.g., Batson, 2009; Epley & Caruso, 2009). Interestingly, Konrath, O'Brien, and Hsing (2011) provided evidence that perspective taking among young adults has been declining over the past 30 years—the same time frame in which selfishness has been progressively increasing.

51. These five items are from a longer selfishness questionnaire developed by Phares and Erskine (1984). For those interested in the complete Selfism Scale (along with scoring), please see Janda (1996).
52. In summarizing research on the importance of non-verbal communication, Wood (2012) reported that, at most, 35 percent of the meaning derived from communication is based upon the verbal content of the message that is spoken. Furthermore, she reported and that up to 90 percent of the meaning is extracted from the many non-verbal components of the communication.

The Best Version of You

53. As a result of her review of the research, Cutrona (2004) concluding that "good marriages require good people" (p. 994). As Vohs, Finkenauer, and Baumeister (2011) put it: "Some traits are inherently adaptive or maladaptive for relationships. Hence, the less of them (destructive traits) or the more of them (beneficial traits) across partners, the better" (p. 139).
54. Bok (2010) and Graham (2012) have reviewed the burgeoning field of happiness research, and they have both come to the clear conclusion that increased wealth does not make one happy. In fact, a study by Quoidbach, Dunn, Petrides, and Mikolajczak (2010) suggested that increased wealth may actually serve to undermine happiness. Similarly, age, health, education, race, and gender impact people's happiness less than does a successful marriage (see also: Bradbury & Karney, 2010; Myers, 1992; Seligman, 2002).

55. Aron, Aron, and Norman (2004) proposed a self-expansion model of romantic relationships. This model posits that a person's motivational and cognitive perspectives can be expanded by forming and maintaining close relationships. For research supporting this model, see Aron, Ketay, Riela, and Aron (2008), Aron, Steele, Kashdan, and Perex (2006), Baxter and West (2003), and Graziano and Bruce (2008).
56. Two of the early pioneers in marriage and family therapy, Carl Whitaker and Augustus Napier, suggested that the experience of marriage can sometimes be akin to a crucible (see their book titled *The Family Crucible*). In this book, Whitaker and Napier have presented numerous examples of how psychological, emotional, financial, and interpersonal "heat" can emerge within the family milieu, and how this experience of heat can bring to the surface a variety of maladaptive personal traits.
57. Whitehead and Popenoe (2001) reported that when a representative national sample of over 1,000 young men and women were surveyed, 94 percent of the never-married singles agreed with the following statement: "When you marry you want your spouse to be your soul mate, first and foremost" (p. 1). Follow-up interviews revealed that for many of these young men and women, implicit in their search for a soul mate was the desire to find someone who would not be expecting them to change in any significant ways.
58. For further discussion of the "three questions of change," see Buri (2006).
59. Numerous authors have emphasized the fact that if you want a stable and satisfying marriage, then you and your spouse should have a desire to change and to grow throughout the marriage process (e.g., Bloom & Bloom, 2004; Davisson & Davisson, 2010; Fincham, Stanley, & Beach, 2007; Fowers, 2000; Howell & Jones, 2010; Sternberg, 1991; Wallerstein & Blakeslee, 1995).

Friendship: The Foundation of Marriage

60. Readers who are interested in practical books that will help them further develop the skills of communication, negotiation, compromise, and conflict resolution, see: Alexander, 2013; Bernstein and Magee (2003), Markman and Stanley (2003), Markman, Stanley, and Blumberg (2010), McKay, Davis, and Fanning (2009), McKay, Fanning, and Paleg (2006), and Robinson (2012).
61. The quote paraphrased here is by Carl Schurz. It reads: "Ideals are like the stars; we never reach them, but like the mariners of the sea, we chart our course by them."
62. When happy couples are contrasted with unhappy couples, one of the primary differences that has been found repeatedly is in the area of communication—unhappy couples do not communicate as often or as effectively as happy couples. For extensive reviews of this literature, see Lauer and Lauer (2009), Olson and Olson (2000), and Williams, Sawyer, and Wahlstrom (2009).
63. Research has revealed that marital boredom is highly predictive of marital dissatisfaction (e.g., Bao & Lyubomirsky, 2013; Tsapelas, Aron, & Orbuch, 2009), and advances in neuroscience have allowed us to determine that at least a part of this boredom can be explained by the biochemistry of the brain. Injecting novelty into one's date nights (even for couples who have been married for many years) will elicit a response in the same brain circuits (involving, for example, dopamine and norepinephrine) as is the case for new romantic relationships (e.g., Aron, 2006; Strong & Aron, 2006).
64. It was Aristotle who first suggested the term "Friend of Virtue" (see *Nicomachean Ethics*).
65. These findings were reported from Linda J. Waite's tabulations of the wave 1 (1987–1988) and wave 2 (1992–1994) data from the National Survey of Families and Households. Waite

and Gallagher (2000) described these findings in this way: "While we tend to talk about bad marriages as if they were permanent things, research suggests that marriage is a dynamic relationship; even the unhappiest of couples who grimly stick it out for the sake of the children can find happiness together a few years down the road. How many unhappy couples turn their marriages around? The truth is shocking: 86 percent of unhappily married people who stick it out find that, five years later, their marriages are happier…The very worst marriages showed the most dramatic turnarounds: 77 percent of the stably married people who rated their marriage as very unhappy (1 on a scale of 1 to 7) in the late eighties said that the same marriage was either "very happy" or "quite happy" five years later" (p. 148).

Marshmallows and Marriages

66. The marshmallow study was originally reported in an article by Shoda, Mischel, and Peake (1990).
67. Goleman (1995) has provided considerable detail surrounding the original marshmallow study. The quote (in *Intentional Dating)* describing the one-marshmallow versus the two-marshmallow children was offered by Goleman (p. 131).
68. These three forced-choice items are from a questionnaire called the Internal-External Locus of Control Scale (Rotter, 1966). Those people who agree with the first alternatives presented in these forced-choice items are more Internal in their Locus of Control, whereas those who are more inclined to agree with the second alternatives are more External. For anyone interested in completing a version of the Internal-External Locus of Control Scale (along with scoring), please see http://www.mindtools.com/pages/article/newCDV_90.htm.

69. Love (2001) stated that "the percentage of people who reported being 'very happy' in their marriage fell from 53.5 percent in the years from 1973–1976 to 37.8 percent in 1996" (p. 16). Furthermore, Popenoe and Defoe-Whitehead (1999) stated: "It is estimated that after 10 years of marriage, only 25 percent of first marriages are successful, that is, still both intact and reportedly happy" (p. 12). Similarly, Knox and Schacht (2008) reported that approximately 20 percent of marriages can be classified as very happy.
70. Scarf (2008) used previous research studies to deduce four reasons why marriages fail. The first three reasons that have been presented here (i.e., unhealthy personal traits, behaving badly, and difficult circumstances) have been derived from Scarf's summary. The fourth reason presented in *Intentional Dating* (i.e., failure to keep the love alive), however, has been expanded from Scarf's work. She had stated that the fourth reason for marriage failure was poor communication by husbands. The fourth reason presented here was expanded to incorporate the work of a much broader range of marriage researchers and therapists who have reported that the failure to keep the love alive leads to the demise of many marriages. For an expanded listing of relevant references germane to keeping the love alive in a marriage, see Buri's (2006) book titled *How to Love Your Wife*.
71. For those interested in further reading about the connections between the four reasons why marriages fail and the traits of one-marshmallow versus two-marshmallow people, the following books and research articles will provide a wealth of information: Alexander (2010), Baker and McNulty (2010), Baumeister, Heatherton, and Tice (1994), Baumgardner and Crothers (2009), Cervone (2000), Doherty (2013), Fincham, Stanley, and Beach (2007), Fowers (2000), Halford, Wilson, Lizzio, and Moore (2002), Knox and Schacht (2008), and Revenson, Kayser, and Bodenmann (2005).

On a personal research note, let me describe one of the studies we have been working on here at the University of St. Thomas. Imagine that you were given the following scenario:

"John and Kari have been married for a little over two years now. During much of this time, they have found that they have a lot in common, that they like a lot of the same activities, and that they enjoy each other's company a lot. Recently, however, John and Kari have begun to notice several areas of disagreement in their relationship. They argue quite a bit about a variety of topics, and sometimes these disagreements have become quite heated. It has recently become increasingly clear that although John and Kari have several things in common, they also have some differences that are creating problems in their relationship."

Now imagine that you were asked to respond to the following two questions on this 6-point scale:

1=Strongly Disagree 2=Disagree Somewhat 3=Disagree

4=Agree 5=Agree Somewhat 6=Strongly Agree

If John and Kari decide to stay together and to work on their relationship, how likely is it that they will be happy with each other in the long run?

If you found *yourself* in a situation like John and Kari's, how likely is it that you would stay in the relationship and try to work out your differences?

Do you think there is a difference in how one-marshmallow people respond to these two questions versus how two-marshmallow people do? The answer is yes.

What we have found is that when we compare those young adults with an External Locus of Control (the one-marshmallow individuals) versus those who have an Internal Locus of Control (the two-marshmallow individuals), those with an External Locus of Control are much more likely to respond that John and Kari will not be happy if they stay in the relationship. Furthermore, they respond that they themselves would be less likely to stay in such a marriage.

Even before personally experiencing marriage, some individuals (one-marshmallow people) are more apt to view happiness after conflict as more difficult to re-capture and they are more apt to predict that they themselves would leave a marriage in which there is conflict. One-marshmallow people have not learned to persist through those circumstances that have failed to immediately work out as they had hoped, and this failure to persist can then impact their attitudes toward working through difficulties in a marriage.

72. If you are interested in the increasing prevalence of the one-marshmallow way of thinking and acting within our culture, see Levine (2008), Marano (2008), and Twenge (2006). In fact, Twenge, Zhang, and Im (2004) have presented empirical evidence that "the average college student in 2002 had a more External Locus of Control than 80 percent of college students in the early 1960s" (p. 308).
73. Wegscheider-Cruse (1989) offered the following (edited) explanation of enabling: "Even at a relatively early stage, people's behaviors are already becoming so unhealthy and irresponsible that the natural consequences of those behaviors threaten to overwhelm them—if they should have to face them. But they rarely do. The people around them, especially those who love them or whose well-being is bound up with theirs, step in and protect them from those consequences. As the problem behaviors progress, enablers step in more often and with more elaborate protection. The effect is to deflect the hand of fate and soften its blow...They pinch-hit for them, hide their mistakes, alibi or lie for them (even to themselves)...An enabling person often acts out of a sincere, if misguided, sense of love and loyalty...Most enablers I have known do not even see their actions as choices; they honestly feel they have no alternatives. 'If I didn't take over,

who would?'" (pp. 89–90). For those readers who would like to better understand the dynamics behind enabling behavior (and what to do to change it), please see: *The Intimacy Factor* (by Pia Mellody and Lawrence Freundlich), *How to Break Your Addiction to a Person* (by Howard Halpern), and *Is It Love or Is It Addiction?* (by Brenda Schaeffer).

74. Citing various studies, Glass (2003) reported that approximately 44 percent of husbands and 25 percent of wives have had at least one affair. Similarly, Haltzman (author of the book titled *The Secrets of Happily Married Men*) stated that by the age of forty-five, two out of every five married men and one out of every five married women have had sex with someone other than their spouse. Infidelity has been reported as the most common reason for divorce (see Amato & Previti, 2003).
75. The title of the book by Chip and Dan Heath is *Switch: How to Change Things When Change Is Hard* (2010).

Why Marshmallows Continue to Matter

76. Gottman and his colleagues (e.g., Gottman, 1994; Gottman, Coan, Carrere, & Swanson, 1998; Gottman & Silver, 1999) reported that a high ratio of positive-to-negative exchanges between husbands and wives is strongly predictive of happy marriages. He has pointed out that a ratio of 5:1 (or higher) is optimal. The probability that a couple who maintains such a ratio will have a happy marriage is nearly 95 percent. Gottman (1994) explained this simple key to having a stable and satisfying marriage this way: "Amazingly, we have found that it all comes down to a simple mathematical formula: no matter what style your marriage follows, you must have at least five times as many positive as negative moments together" (p. 29).

77. Based on extensive research, Gottman and Silver (1999) reported that it is most often (i.e., 80 percent of the time) the wife who brings up difficult topics in the marriage.
78. In summarizing the research on criticism and marital success, several authors have asserted that criticism (more often by the wife) is the most consistent factor that differentiates distressed couples from non-distressed couples (e.g., Christensen & Walczynski, 1997; Notarius, Benson, Sloane, Vanzetti, & Hornyak, 1989; Notarius & Pelligrini, 1987).
79. For more information on the distinctions between criticism and a complaint, see Gottman (1999) and Gottman and Silver (1999).
80. Authors have begun to understand how a sense of failure can trigger feelings of shame, and this appears to be especially true for men. For two particularly accessible books discussing this topic, see Brown (2012) and Love and Stosny (2008). These authors have clarified how criticism from one's wife can trigger feelings of shame in a man.
81. For discussions of the relationship between communication and marital success, see Benokraitis (2011), DeGenova, Stinnett, and Stinnett (2011), Galvin, Bylund, and Brommel (2011), and Welch (2010).
82. Communication consists of talking (and listening) at progressively deeper levels. The deeper you go, the greater the intimacy in the relationship. There are essentially four levels of communication, and if a couple wants to experience intimacy in their relationship, then they should strive for communication on all four levels.

    Level 1: Superficial Conversation. Admittedly, this first level of communication is not very deep. It is the chitchat and the small talk of our day-to-day interactions. It's the "How ya doin'" and "How's your day goin'" type of comments.

    Level 2: People, Places, Things. This is a very factual level of communication. It consists of talking about those people, places, and things that consume most of our waking moments. It is an interesting exercise to take note of just how much time we spend each day talking about the people at work who irritate us, the sports team we're interested in, the latest fashions, the chores around the house that need to be done, who's who in the world of entertainment, the vacation we took (and the one we are planning to take), the old friend we ran into at the mall, the weather... This level of communication is at the heart of report-talk, and it is admittedly an important part of communication; it is important to let someone we love know what irritates us, what we enjoy, the activities we are planning, and how we spend our time. But this is still a relatively superficial type of communication.

Level 3: What We Care About. When we communicate at this level, we are letting the other person know what we care about, what we value, what is important to us, what we believe in, and what matters to us. If a couple fails to regularly get to Level 3, then their communication has stalled at a fairly superficial level. The intimacy with which love grows is dependent upon Level 3 communication. For any couple who struggles to communicate at this level, I would suggest getting a book of questions that you can use to jump-start your discussions. The book I most often recommend for this purpose is: *If Questions for the Soul* by Evelyn McFarlane and James Saywell.

Level 4: The Personal Impact of Events. This level of communication occurs when we reveal to another person just how an event has impacted us personally; in other words, how a circumstance we are facing has moved us, or how we have been affected (pleasantly, unpleasantly, or both) by an event in our lives. As an example, when one of my sons and his wife recently experienced a miscarriage, my son freely talked about how this was impacting him personally. He talked about the sadness, the pain, the disappointment, the child that he would never know, the hope for another baby in the future, and the doubts. It should never be taken lightly when someone communicates with us at this level, and such deep communication is at the heart of intimacy.

For anyone who would like a more detailed discussion of these four levels of communication, see Buri (2006).

"How Do I Love Thee? Let Me Count the Ways…"

83. The title of this chapter is taken from the poem written by Elizabeth Barrett Browning.
84. Over a hundred years ago, William James (1890) stated (in his seminal work titled *The Principles of Psychology*): "The deepest principle in human nature is the craving to be appreciated" (p. 313). For research addressing the effects of fondness and appreciation on relationships (in general) and marriages (in particular) see Caughlin and Huston (2006), Cordova, Gee, and Warren (2005), Fagley (2012), Fredrickson (2004), Gordon, Arnette, and Smith (2011); Gottman and Levenson (1999), Gottman, Ryan, Carrere, and Erley (2002), Gottman and Silver (2012), Huston and Melz (2004), Lambert, Clark, Durtschi, Fincham, and Graham (2010), Seligman (2002), and Tsang, Rowatt, and Buechsel (2008).

Gratitude

85. Barry Schwartz developed the Maximizer/Satisficer Questionnaire. For more information about this questionnaire and some of the research findings that have emerged from the use of this scale, see Schwartz (2000, 2004), Schwartz and Ward (2004), and Schwartz, Ward, Monterosso, Lyubomirsky, White, and Lehman (2002).
86. Young adults at the University of St. Thomas were asked the extent to which they agreed with statements like the following: "If I get married and we encounter rough times

in our marriage, I will no doubt miss the life I have had as a single person" and "Most people have to give up way too much to make a marriage work." In all, there were seven such statements, and the responses to all seven items constituted the Marriage Ambivalence score for each young man or woman. When comparing the Marriage Ambivalence of Maximizers versus Satisficers, Maximizers scored significantly higher.

87. In other studies completed here at the University of St. Thomas, college students who were in serious dating relationships were asked to complete a questionnaire measuring how much of the three primary components of love (Sternberg, 2004)—Intimacy, Passion, and Commitment—they were experiencing with their current partner. Following are sample questionnaire items for each: "My partner and I self-disclose private thoughts and information to each other" (Intimacy), "My partner and I are very affectionate toward each other" (Passion), and "I think of our relationship as a permanent one" (Commitment). When comparing Maximizers versus Satisficers, Maximizers reported significantly lower Intimacy, Passion, and Commitment toward their partner.
88. Maximizers who are in serious relationships also have been found to be more attentive to potential partners other than the person they are currently dating. Furthermore, Maximizers have a much more positive attitude toward divorce. Further details about these research findings can be found in Buri, Brelje, Gunty, and Arola (2010) and Buri, Gunty, and King (2008).
89. The complete Maximizer Scale can be found in Schwartz's book, *The Paradox of Choice*. It is also available at the following website: http://betweenlivingandexisting.blogspot.com/2008/08/maximizer-versus-satisficer.html.
90. In our research here at the University of St. Thomas, we have found that Maximizers are significantly less grateful than are Satisficers.

91. These proverbs were provided by Emmons and Hill (2001).
92. For a detailed description of studies investigating the effects of gratitude, see Robert Emmons' (2007) book titled *Thanks! How the New Science of Gratitude Can Make You Happier.*
93. For more information on the role of attributions in marital functioning (as well as discussions of how personal sensitivities can influence a person's attributions), see Bradbury and Karney (2004, 2010), Dattilio (2010), DeGenova (2008), Epstein and Baucom (2002), Fincham (2003), Finkel, Slotter, Luchies, Walton, and Gross (2013), and Notarius, Lashley, and Sullivan (1997).
94. For those readers interested in research confirming the importance of forgiveness for successful marriages, see Carlisle, Tsang, Ahmad, Worthington, vanOyen, and Wade (2012), Enright and Fitzgibbons (2002), Fincham (2010), Fincham, Hall, and Beach (2005, 2006), and Miller, Worthington, Hook, Davis, Gartner, and Frohne (2013).
95. The Heartland Forgiveness Scale was originally published by Thompson, Snyder, Hoffman, Michael, Rasmussen, Billings, Heinze, Neufeld, Shorey, Roberts, and Roberts (2005).

    The scale (as well as scoring information) can be found at the following website: http://digitalcommons.unl.edu/cgi/viewcontent.cgi?article=1451&context=psychfacpub. This scale will allow you to determine how forgiving you are of others, how forgiving you are of yourself, and how easily you are able to arrive at forgiveness for difficult situations.

The Love Bank

96. If you want to learn more about Willard Harley's analogy of the Love Bank, see Harley (2001, 2009).

References

Adams, Mike. *Natural Health Solutions.* NY: Incubation Books, 2006.

Alexander, Susanne M. *All-in-One Marriage Prep.* Naples, FL: Barringer, 2010.

Alexander, Susanne M. *Deciding in Unity: A Practical Process for Married Couples to Agree on Practically Everything.* Chattanooga, TN: Marriage Transformation Press, 2013

Amato, Paul R., and Denise Previti. "People's Reasons for Divorce." *Journal of Family Issues* 24 (2003): 602-626.

Antonucci, Toni C., Kira S. Birditt, and Kristine J. Ajrouch. "Social Relationships and Aging." In *Handbook of Psychology, Vol. 6: Developmental Psychology,* edited by Richard M. Lerner, M. Ann Easterbrooks, Jayanthi Mistry, and Irving B. Weiner, 495-514. Hoboken, NJ: Wiley.

Aron, Arthur. "Relationship Neuroscience: Advancing the Social Psychology of Close Relationships Using Functional Neuroimaging." In *Bridging Social Psychology: Benefits of Transdisciplinary Approaches,* edited by Paul A. M. Lange, 261-266. Mahwah, NJ: Lawrence Erlbaum.

Aron, Arthur, Elaine N. Aron, and Christina Norman. "The Self-Expansion Model of Motivation and Cognition in Close Relationships and Beyond." In *Blackwell Handbook in Social Psychology: Interpersonal Processes,* edited by Marilyn B. Brewer and Miles Hewstone, 99-123. NY: Wiley-Blackwell.

Aron, Arthur, Helen Fisher, Debra J. Mashek, Greg Strong, Haifang Li, and Lucy L. Brown. "Reward, Motivation, and Emotion Systems Associated with Early-Stage Intense Romantic Love." *Journal of Neurophysiology* 94 (2005): 327-337.

Aron, Arthur, Sarah Ketay, Suzanne Riela, and Elaine N. Aron. "How Close Others Construct and Reconstruct Who We Are and How We Feel About Ourselves." In *The Self and Social Relationships,* edited by Joanne V. Wood, Abraham Tesser, and John G. Holmes, 209-229. NY: Psychology Press.

Aron, Arthur, Jodie L. Steele, Todd B. Kashdan, and Max Perez. "When Similars Do Not Attract: Tests of a Prediction from the Self-Expansion Model." *Personal Relationships* 13 (2006): 387-396.

Bahr, Howard M., and Kathleen S. Bahr. "Families and Self-Sacrifice." *Social Forces* 79 (2001): 1231-1258.

Baker, Levi L., and James K. McNulty. "Shyness and Marriage." *Personality and Social Psychology Bulletin* 36 (2010): 665-676.

Baker, Levi L., James K. McNulty, Nickola C. Overall, Nathaniel M. Lambert, and Frank D. Fincham. "How Do Relationship Maintenance Behaviors Affect Individual Well-Being?: A Contextual Perspective." *Social Psychological and Personality Science* 4 (2013): 282-289.

Bao, Katherine J., and Sonja Lyubomirsky. "Making It Last: Combating Hedonic Adaptation in Romantic Relationships." *Journal of Positive Psychology* 8 (2013): 196-206.

Bartels, Andreas, and Semir Zeki. "The Neural Basis of Romantic Love." *NeuroReport* 11 (2000): 3829-2834.

Batson, Daniel C. "Two Forms of Perspective Taking: Imagining How Another Feels and Imagining How You Would Feel." In *Handbook of Imagination and Mental Simulation*, edited by Keith D. Markman, William M. P. Klein, and Julie A. Suhr, 267-279. NY: Psychology Press.

Baumeister, Roy F., Todd F. Heatherton, and Diane M. Tice. *Losing Control.* San Diego, CA: Academic Press, 1994.

Baumeister, Roy F., and John Tierney. *Willpower: Rediscovering the Greatest Human Strength.* NY: Penguin Books, 2011.

Baumgardner, Steve R., and Marie K. Crothers. *Positive Psychology.* Upper Saddle River, NJ: Prentice Hall.

Baxter, Leslie A., and Lee West. "Couple Perceptions of Their Similarities and Differences: A Dialectic Perspective. *Journal of Social and Personal Relationships* 20 (2003): 491-514.

Benokraitis, Nijole V. *Marriages and Families: Changes, Choices, and Constraints.* NY: Prentice Hall, 2011.

Bernstein, Jeffrey, and Susan Magee. *Why Can't You Read My Mind?* Boston, MA: Da Capo Press, 2003.

Bloom, Linda, and Charlie Bloom. *101 Things I Wish I Knew When I Got Married.* Novato, CA: New World Library, 2004.

Bok, Derek. *The Politics of Happiness: What Government Can Learn From the New Research On Well-Being.* Princeton, MA: Princeton University Press, 2010.

Bradbury, Thomas N., and Benjamin R. Karney. "Understanding and Altering the Longitudinal Course of Marriage." *Journal of Marriage and Family* 66 (2004): 862-879.

Bradbury, Thomas N., and Benjamin R. Karney. *Intimate Relationships.* NY: Norton, 2010.

Bradshaw, John. *Healing the Shame That Binds You.* Scottsdale, AZ: HCI Press, 2005.

Brown, Brene. *Daring Greatly.* Los Angeles, CA: Gotham Press, 2012.

Brown, David. "A Sweeping Survey of Americans' Sexual Behavior." *The Washington Post,* March 4, 2011.

Brown, Sandra L. *Women Who Love Psychopaths.* NY: Mask Publishing, 2010.

Buehlman, Kim T., John M. Gottman, and Lynn F. Katz. "How a Couple Views Their Past Predicts Their Future." *Journal of Family Psychology* 5 (1992): 295-318.

Buri, John R. *How to Love Your Wife.* Mustang, OK: Tate, 2006.

Buri, John R., Amy L. Gunty, and Stephanie L. King. "Should I Stay Or Should I Go?: Maximizers Versus Satisficers." Paper presented at the 116th annual meeting of the American Psychological Association, Boston, August, 2008.

Buri, John R., Heather L. Brelje, Amy L. Gunty, and Nicole T. Arola. *Maximizers Versus Satisficers: Differences in Romanic Love Choices.* Paper presented at the 118th annual meeting of the American Psychological Association, San Diego, August, 2010.

Buyukcan-Tetik, Asuman, Catrin Finkenaueer, Safie Kuppens, and Kathleen D. Vohs. "Both Trust and Self-Control Are Necessary to Prevent Intrusive Behaviors: Evidence from a Longitudinal Study of Married Couples." *Journal of Family Psychology* 27 (2013): 671-676.

Campbell, W. Keith. *When You Are in Love With a Man Who Loves Himself.* Naperville, IL: Sourcebooks Casablanca, 2005.

Campbell, W. Keith, and Joshua D. Miller. *The Handbook of Narcissism and Narcissistic Personality Disorder: Theoretical Approaches, Empirical Findings, and Treatments.* Hoboken, NJ: Wiley, 2011.

Canary, Daniel J., and Marianne M. Dainton. "Maintaining Relationships." In *The Cambridge Handbook of Personal Relationships,* edited by Anita L. Vangelistic and Daniel Perlman, 727-743. NY: Cambridge University Press, 2006.

Canary, Daniel J., Laura Stafford, and Beth A. Semic. "A Panel Study of Associations Between Maintenance Strategies and Relational Characteristics." *Journal of Marriage and Family* 64 (2002): 395-406.

Carlisle, Robert D., Jo-Ann Tsang, Nadia Y. Ahmad, Everett L. Worthington, Charlotte Witvliet vanOyen, and Nathaniel Wade. "Do Actions Speak Louder Than Words?: Differential Effects of Apology and Restitution on Behavioral and Self-Report Measures of Forgiveness." *Journal of Positive Psychology,* 7 (2012): 294-305.

Caughlin, John P., and Ted L. Huston. "The Affective Structure of Marriage." In *The Cambridge Handbook of Personal Relationships,* edited by Anita L. Vangelisti and Daniel Perlman, 131- 155. NY: Cambridge University Press, 2006.

Caughlin, John P., Ted L. Huston, and Renate M. Houts. "How Does Personality Matter in Marriage?: An Examination of Trait Anxiety, Interpersonal Negativity, and Marital Satisfaction." *Journal of Personality and Social Psychology* 78 (2000): 326-336.

Cervone, Daniel. "Thinking About Self-Efficacy." *Behavior Modification* 24 (2000): 30-56.

Chapman, Gary. *The Five Love Languages.* Chicago: Northfield Publishing, 2004.

Christensen, Andrew, and Pamela T. Walczynski. "Conflict and Satisfaction in Couples." In *Satisfaction in Close Relationships* edited by Robert J. Sternberg and Mahzad Hojjat, 249-274. NY: Guilford, 1997.

Clements, Mari L., Scott M. Stanley, and Howard J. Markman. "Before They Said I Do: Discriminating Among Marital Outcomes Over 13 Years." *Journal of Marriage and Family* 66 (2004): 613-626.

Cole, Tim. "Deception Confidence in Romantic Relationships: Confidently Lying to the One You Love." In *Advances in Psychology Research,* edited by Serge P. Shohov, 127-139. Hauppauge, NY: Nova Science Publishers, 2005.

Conkle, Andrew. "Scientific Insights from 21st Century Dating." *APS Observer* 23 (2010): 12- 26.

Cordova, James V., Christina B. Gee, and Lisa Z. Warren. "Emotional Skillfulness in Marriage." *Journal of Social and Clinical Psychology* 24 (2005): 218-235.

Covey, Stephen R. *The Seven Habits of Highly Effective People.* NY: Simon and Shuster, 1989.

Cox, Frank D., and Kevin Demmitt. *Human Intimacy.* NY: Wadsworth, 2014.

Creasey, Gary, and Patricia Jarvis. "Attachment and Marriage." In *Handbook of Research on Adult Learning and Development,* edited by M. Cecit Smith and Nancy DeFrates-Densch, 269-304. NY: Routledge / Taylor and Francis, 2009.

Curtis, Thomas J., Yan Liu, Brandon J. Aragona, and Zuoxin Wang. "Dopamine and Monogamy." *Brain Research* 1126 (2006): 76-90.

Cutrona, Carolyn E. "A Psychological Perspective: Marriage and the Social Provisions of Relationships." *Journal of Marriage and Family* 66 (2004): 992-999.

Dalton, Jane E. "Increasing Marital Satisfaction in Clinically Distressed Couples: The Role of Empathic Accuracy and We-ness." PhD diss., York University, 2007.

Dattilia, Frank M. *Cognitive-Behavioral Therapy with Couples and Families.* NY: Guilford, 2010.

Davisson, Joel, and Kathy Davisson. "Six Keys to an Outrageously Happy Marriage." In *All-in- One Marriage Prep,* edited by Susanne M. Alexander, 318-322. Naples, FL: Barringer.

Debrot, Anik, Dominik Schoebi, Meinrad Perrex, and Andrea B. Horn. "Touch as an Interpersonal Emotion Regulation Process in Couples' Daily Lives: The Mediating Role of Psychological Intimacy." *Personality and Social Psychology Bulletin* 39 (2013): 1373-1385.

DeGenova, Mary Kay. *Intimate Relationships, Marriages, and Families.* NY: McGraw Hill, 2008.

DeGenova, Mary Kay, Nick Stinnett, and Nancy Stinnett. *Intimate Relationships.* NY: McGraw Hill, 2011.

Doherty, William J. *Take Back Your Marriage: Sticking Together in a World That Pulls Us Apart.* NY: Guilford, 2013.

Emmons, Robert A. *Thanks! How the New Science of Gratitude Can Make You Happier.* NY: Houghton Mifflin, 2007.

Emmons, Robert A., and Joanna Hill. *Words of Gratitude.* Philadelphia, PA: Templeton Foundation Press, 2001.

Enright, Robert D., and Richard P. Fitzgibbons. *Helping Clients Forgive: An Empirical Guide for Resolving Anger and Restoring Hope.* Washington, DC: American Psychological Association, 2002.

Epley, Nicholas, and Eugene M. Caruso. "Perspective Taking: Misstepping Into Others' Shoes." In *Handbook of Imagination and Mental Simulation,* edited by Keith D. Markman, William M. P. Klein, and Julie A. Suhr, 295-309. NY: Psychology Press, 2009.

Epstein, Norman B., and Donald H. Baucom. "*Enhanced Cognitive-Behavioral Therapy for Couples.* Washington, DC: American Psychological Association, 2002.

Eshelman, Ross. *The Family.* Boston, MA: Allyn and Bacon, 2003.

Fagley, N. S. "Appreciation Uniquely Predicts Life Satisfaction Above Demographics, the Big 5 Personality Factors, and Gratitude." *Personality and Individual Differences* 53 (2012): 59-63.

Fincham, Frank D. "Marital Conflict: Correlates, Structure, and Context." *Current Directions in Psychological Science* 12 (2003): 23-27.

Fincham, Frank D. "Forgiveness: Integral to a Science of Close Relationships." In *Prosocial Motives, Emotions, and Behavior: The Better Angels of Our Nature,* edited by Mario Mikulincer and Phillip R. Shaver, 347-365. Washington, DC: American Psychological Association, 2010.

Fincham, Frank D., Julie Hall, and Steven R. H. Beach. "'Til Lack of Forgiveness Doth Us Part: Forgiveness in Marriage."

In *Handbook of Forgiveness*, edited by Everett L. Worthington, 207-226. NY: Routledge, 2005.

Fincham, Frank D., Julie Hall, and Steven R. H. Beach. "Forgiveness in Marriage: Current Status and Future Directions." *Family Relations* 55 (2006): 415-427.

Fincham, Frank D., Scott M. Stanley, and Steven R. H, Beach. "Transformational Processes in Marriage: An Analysis of Emerging Trends." *Journal of Marriage and Family* 69 (2007): 275- 292.

Finkel, Eli J., and W. Keith Campbell. "Self-"Control and Accommodation in Relationships." *Journal of Personality and Social Psychology* 81 (2001): 263-277.

Finkel, Eli J., Paul W. Eastwick, Benjamin R. Karney, Harry T. Reis, and Susan Sprecher. "Online Dating: A Critical Analysis from the Perspective of Psychological Science." *Psychological Science in the Public Interest* 13 (2012): 3-66.

Finkel, Eli J., Erica B. Slotter, Laura B. Luchies, Gregory M. Walton, and James J. Gross. "A Brief Intervention to Promote Conflict Reappraisal Preserves Marital Quality Over Time." *Psychological Science* 24 (2013): 1595-1601.

Fowers, Blaine J. *Beyond the Myth of Marital Happiness.* San Francisco, CA: Jossey-Bass, 2000.

Fredrickson, Barbara L. "Gratitude, Like Other Positive Emotions, Broadens and Builds." In *The Psychology of Gratitude,* edited by Robert A. Emmons and Michael E. McCullough, 145-166. NY: Oxford University Press, 2004.

Galvin, Kathleen M., Carma L. Bylund, and Bernard Brommel. *Family Communication.* NY: Allyn and Bacon, 2011.

Ganiban, Jody M., Erica L. Spotts, Paul Lichtenstein, Gagan S. Khera, David Reiss, and Jenae M. Neiderhiser. "Can Genetic Factors Explain the Spillover of Warmth and Negativity Across Family Relationships?" *Twin Research and Human Genetics* 10 (2007): 299-313.

Gag, Wanda, trans. *Snow White and the Seven Dwarfs.* NY: Smithmark Publishers, 1999.

Glass, Shirley P. *Not "Just Friends."* NY: Free Press, 2003.

Glenn, Norval D., Jeremy Uecker, and Robert Love. "Later First marriage and Marital Success." *Social Science Research* 39 (2010): 787-800.

Goleman, Daniel. *Emotional Intelligence.* NY: Bantam Books, 1995.

Goode, William J. "The Theoretical Importance of Love." *American Sociological Review* 24 (1959): 38-47.

Gordon, Cameron L., Robyn A. M. Arnette, and Rachel E. Smith. "Have You Thanked Your Spouse Today?" *Personality and Individual Differences* 50 (2011): 339-343.

Gottman, John M. *Why Marriages Succeed or Fail...and How You Can Make Yours Last.* NY: Simon and Schuster, 1994.

Gottman, John M. *The Marriage Clinic: A Scientifically-Based Marital Therapy.* NY: Norton, 1999.

Gottman, John M., James Coan, Sybil Carrere, and Catherine Swanson. "Predicting Marital Happiness and Stability from Newlywed Interactions." *Journal of Marriage and Family* 60 (1998): 5-22.

Gottman, John M., and Joan DeClaire. *The Relationship Cure.* NY: Crown, 2002.

Gottman, John M., Julie Schwartz Gottman, and Joan DeClaire. *Ten Lessons to Transform Your Marriage.* NY: Crown, 2006.

Gottman, John M., and Robert W. Levenson. "What Predicts Change in Marital Interaction Over Time?" *Family Process* 38 (1999): 143-158.

Gottman, John M., Kimberly D. Ryan, Sybil Carrere, and Annette M. Erley. "Toward a Scientifically-Based Marital Therapy." In *Family Psychology,* edited by Howard A. Liddle, Daniel A. Santisteban, Ronald F. Levant, and James H. Bray, 147-174. Washington, DC: American Psychological Association, 2002.

Gottman, John M., and Nan Silver. *The Seven Principles for making Marriage Work.* NY: Three Rivers Press, 1999.

Gottman, John M., and Nan Silver. *What Makes Love Last: How To Build Trust and Avoid Betrayal.* NY: Simon and Schuster, 2012.

Goulston, Mark, and Philip Goldberg. *The Six Secrets of a Lasting Relationship.* NY: Putnam, 2002.

Graham, Carol. *Happiness Around the World: The Paradox of Happy Peasants and Miserable Millionaires.* NY: Oxford University Press, 2012.

Graziano, William G., and Jennifer W. Bruce. "Attraction and the Initiation of Relationships: A Review of Empirical Literature." In *Handbook of Relationship Initiation,* edited by Susan Sprecher, Amy Wenzel, and John Harvey, 269-295. NY: Psychology Press, 2008.

Gunther, Randi. *Relationship Saboteurs: Overcoming the Ten Behaviors that Undermine Love.* Oakland, CA: New Harbinger, 2010.

Halford, W. Kim, Keithia L. Wilson, Alf Lizzio, and Elizabeth Moore. "Does Working At a Relationship Work?: Relationship Self-Regulation and Relationship Outcomes." In *Understanding Marriage: Developments in the Study of Couple Interaction,* edited by Patricia Noller and Judith A. Feeney, 493-517. NY: Cambridge University Press, 2002.

Halpern, Howard. *How to Break Your Addiction to a Person.* NY: Bantam Books, 2003.

Halpern, Howard. *Cutting Loose.* NY: Fireside, 2005.

Haltzman, Scott. *The Secrets of Happily Married Men.* San Francisco, CA: Jossey-Bass, 2006.

Haltzman, Scott. *The Secrets of Surviving Infidelity.* Baltimore, MD: Johns Hopkins University Press, 2013.

Hardwired to Connect. NY: Institute for American Values, 2003.

Harley, Willard F. *Fall in Love, Stay in Love.* Grand Rapids, MI: Revell, 2001.

Harley, Willard F. *Love Busters; Protecting Your Marriage From Habits that Destroy Romantic Love.* Grand Rapids, MI: Revell, 2008.

Harley, Willard F. *Five Steps to Romantic Love.* Grand Rapids, MI: Revell, 2009.

Harrar, Sari, and Rita DeMaria. *The 7 Stages of Marriage: Laughter, Intimacy, and Passion Today, Tomorrow, Forever.* Pleasantville, NY: Reader's Digest, 2007.

Hatfield, Elaine, and Richard L. Rapson. "Passionate Love and Sexual Behavior: Multidisciplinary Perspectives." In *Social Relationships: Cognitive, Affective, and Motivational Processes,* edited by Joseph P. Forgas and Julie Fitness, 21-37. NY: Psychology Press, 2008.

Heath, Chip, and Dan Heath. *Switch: How to Change Things When Change Is Hard.* NY: Broadway Books, 2010.

Heaton, Tim B. "Factors Contributing to Increasing Marital Stability in the United States." *Journal of Family Issues* 23 (2002): 392-409.

Hemfelt, Robert, Frank Minirth, and Paul Meier. *Love Is a Choice: The Definitive Book on Letting Go of Unhealthy Relationships.* Nashville, TN: Thomas Nelson, 2003.

Hendrick, Clyde, and Susan S. Hendrick. "Styles of Romantic Love." In *The New Psychology of Love,* edited by Robert J. Sternberg and Karin Sternberg, 149-170. New Haven, CT: Yale University Press, 2008.

Hendrix, Harville. *Getting the Love You Want.* NY: Henry Holt, 2007.

Howell, Patty, and Ralph Jones. *World Class Marriage: How to Create the Relationship You Always Wanted With the Partner You Already Have.* NY: Rowman and Littlefield, 2010.

Huston, Ted L., John P. Caughlin, Renate M. Houts, Shanna E. Smith, and Laura J. George. "The Connubial Crucible: Newlywed Years as Predictors of Marital Delight, Distress, and Divorce." *Journal of Personality and Social Psychology* 80 (2001): 237-252.

Huston, Ted L., and Heidi Melz. "The Case for (Promoting) Marriage: The Devil Is in the Details." *Journal of Marriage and Family* 66 (2004): 943-958.

Huston, Ted L., Catherine Surra, Nathaniel Fitzgerald, and Rodney Cate. "From Courtship to Marriage: Mate Selection as an Interpersonal Process." In *Personal Relationships,* edited by Steve Duck, 53-90. London: Academic Press, 1981.

Impett, Emily A., and Amie M. Gordon. "For the Good of Others: Toward a Positive Psychology of Sacrifice." In *Positive Psychology: Exploring the Best in People,* edited by Shane J. Lopez, 79-100. Westport, CT: Praeger, 2008.

James, William. *The Principles of Psychology.* NY: Holt, 1890.

Janda, Louis. *The Psychologist's Book of Self-Tests.* NY: Perigee Books, 1996.

Jankowiak, W. R., and E. F. Fischer. "A Cross-Cultural Perspective on Romantic Love." In *Human Emotions: A Reader,* edited by Jennifer M. Jenkins, Keith Oatley, and Nancy L. Stein, 55-62. NY: Wiley-Blackwell, 1998.

Johnson, Matthew D., Catherine L. Cohan, Joanne Davila, Erika Lawrence, Ronald D. Rogge, Benjamin R. Karney, Kieran T. Sullivan, and Thomas N. Bradbury. "Problem-Solving Skills and Affective Expressions as Predictors of Change in Marital Satisfaction." *Journal of Consulting and Clinical Psychology* 73 (2005): 15-27.

Kayser, Karen. *When Love Dies: The Process of Marital Disaffection.* NY: Guilford, 1993.

Kephart, William M. "Some Correlates of Romantic Love." *Journal of Marriage and Family* 29 (1967): 470-474.

Knapp, Mark L. "Lying and Deception in Close Relationships." In *The Cambridge Handbook of Personal Relationships,* edited by Anita L. Vangelisti and Daniel Perlman, 517-532. NY: Cambridge University Press, 2006.

Knoke, Julia, Julia Burau, and Bernd Roehrle. "Attachment Styles, Loneliness, Quality, and Stability of Marital Relationships." *Journal of Divorce and Remarriage* 51 (2010): 310-325.

Knox, David, and Caroline Schacht. *Choices in Relationships.* Belmont, CA: Wadsworth, 2008.

Konrath, Sara H., Edward H. O'Brien, and Courtney Hsing. "Changes in Dispositional Empathy in American College Students Over Time: A Meta-Analysis." *Personality and Social Psychology Review* 15 (2011): 180-198.

Kurdek, Lawrence A. "The Nature and Predictors of the Trajectory of Change in Marital Quality for Husbands and Wives Over the First 10 Years of Marriage." *Developmental Psychology* 35 (1999): 1283-1296.

Laaser, Debra. *Shattered Vows.* Grand Rapids, MI: Zondervan, 2008.

Lambert, Nathaniel M., Margaret S. Clark, Jared Durtschi, Frank D. Fincham, and Steven M. Graham. "Benefits of Expressing Gratitude." *Psychological Science* 21 (2010): 574-580.

Lantz, Herman R., Margaret Britton, Raymond L. Schmitt, and E. C. Snyder. "Pre-Industrial Patterns in the Colonial Family in America: A Content Analysis of Colonial Magazines." *American Sociological Review* 33 (1968): 413-427.

Lauer, Robert H., and Jeanette C. Lauer. *Marriage and Family: A Quest for Intimacy.* NY: McGraw Hill, 2009.

Laumann, Edward O., John H. Gagnon, Robert T. Michael, and Stuart S. Michaels. *The Social Organization of Sexuality.* Chicago: University of Chicago Press, 1994.

Levine, Madeline. *The Price of Privilege.* NY: Harper, 2008.

Lewis, C. S. *The Screwtape Letters (reprint ed.).* NY: HarperOne, 2009.

Love, Patricia. *The Truth about Love.* NY: Fireside Books, 2001.

Love, Patricia, and Steven Stosny. *How to Improve Your Marriage without Talking About It.* Easton, PA: Harmony Press, 2008.

Mahoney, Annette, Kenneth I. Pargament, Nalini Tarakeshwar, and Aaron B. Swank. "Religion in the Home in the 1980s and 1990s: A Meta-Analytic Review and Conceptual Analysis of Links between Religion, Marriage, and Parenting." *Psychology of Religion and Spirituality* 5 (2008): 63-101.

Marano, Hara Estroff. *A Nation of Wimps.* NY: Broadway Books, 2008.

Markman, Howard, and Scott Stanley. *12 Hours to a Great Marriage: A Step-by-Step Guide for Making Love Last.* San Francisco, CA: Jossey-Bass, 2003.

Markman, Howard, Scott Stanley, and Susan L. Blumberg. *Fighting for Your Marriage.* San Francisco, CA: Jossey-Bass, 1994.

Markman, Howard, Scott Stanley, and Susan L. Blumberg. *Fighting for Your Marriage (revised ed.).* San Francisco: Jossey-Bass, 2010.

McCarthy, Barry, and Emily McCarthy. *Rekindling Desire: A Step-by-Step Program to Help Low-Sex and No-Sex Marriages.* NY: Brunner-Routledge, 2003.

McCarthy, Barry, and Emily McCarthy. *Getting It Right the First Time: Creating a Healthy Marriage.* NY: Brunner-Routledge, 2004.

McFarlane, Evelyn, and James Saywell. *If Questions for the Soul.* NY: Villard, 1998.

McKay, Matthew, Martha Davis, and Patrick Fanning. *Messages: The Communication Skills Book.* Oakland, CA: New Harbinger, 2009.

McKay, Matthew, Patrick Fanning, and Kim Paleg. *Couple Skills.* Oakland, CA: New Harbinger, 2006.

Meier, Ann M. "Adolescents' Transition to First Intercourse, Religiosity, and Attitudes About Sex. *Social Forces* 81 (2003): 1031-1052.

Mellody, Pia, and Lawrence S. Freundlich. *The Intimacy Factor; The Ground Rules for Overcoming the Obstacles to Truth, Respect, and Lasting Love.* San Francisco: Harper, 2004.

Miller, Andrea J., Everett L. Worthington, Joshua N. Hood, Don E. Davis, Aubrey L. Gartner, and Nicole A. Frohne. "Managing Hurt and Disappointment: Improving Communication of Reproach and Apology. *Journal of Mental Health Counseling* 35 (2013): 108-123.

Miller, Rowland, and Daniel Perlman. *Intimate Relationships.* NY: McGraw Hill, 2009.

Montoya, R. Matthew, Robert S. Horton, and Jeffrey Kirchner. "Is Actual Similarity Necessary for Attraction?" *Journal of Social and Personal Relationships* 25 (2008): 889-922.

Myers, David. *The Pursuit of Happiness: Who Is Happy and Why.* NY: William Morrow, 1992.

Myers, David. *Psychology.* NY: Worth, 2013.

Noller, Patricia. "What Is This Thing Called Love?" *Personal Relationships* 3 (1996): 97-115.

Norwood, Robin. *Women Who Love Too Much: When You Keep Wishing and Hoping He'll Change.* NY: Gallery Books, 2008.

Notarius, Clifford I., Paul R. Benson, Douglas Sloane, Nelly A. Vanzetti, and L. M. Hornyak. "Exploring the Interface Between Perception and Behavior: An Analysis of Marital Interaction in Distressed and Nondistressed Couples." *Behavioral Assessment* 11 (1989): 39-64.

Notarius, Clifford I., Samuel L. Lashley, and Debra J. Sullivan. "Angry At Your Partner? Think Again. In *Satisfaction in Close Relationships,* edited by Robert J. Sternberg and Hahzad Hojjat, 219-248. NY: Guilford, 1997.

Notarius, Clifford I., and David S. Pelligrini. "Differences Between Husbands and Wives: Implications for Understanding Marital Discord." In *Understanding Major Mental Disorder: The Contributions of Family Interaction Research,* edited by

Kurt Hahlweg and Michael Goldstein, 231-249. NY: Family Process Press, 1987.

Ogolski, Brian G., and Jill R. Bowers. "A Meta-Analytic Review of Relationship Maintenance and Its Correlates." *Journal of Social and Personal Relationships* 30 (2013): 343-367.

Olson, David H., John DeFrain, and Linda Skogrand. *Marriages and Families.* NY: McGraw Hill, 2011.

Olson, David H., and Amy K. Olson. *Empowering Couples: Building on Your Strengths.* Minneapolis, MN: Life Innovations, 2000.

Ostwald, Martin, trans. *Nicomachean Ethics.* NY: Macmillan, 1962.

Paik, Anthony. "Adolescent Sexuality and the Risk of Marital Dissolution." *Journal of Marriage and Family* 73 (2011): 472-485.

Paloutzian, Raymond F., and Crystal L. Park. *Handbook of the Psychology of Religion and Spirituality.* NY: Guilford, 2013.

Parker-Pope, Tara. "Is It Love Or Mental Illness? They're Closer than You Think." *The Wall Street Journal,* February 13, 2007.

Parker-Pope, Tara. *For Better: The Science of a Good Marriage.* NY: Dutton, 2010.

Patz, Aviva. "Will Your Marriage Last?" In *Annual Editions: The Family,* edited by Kathleen R. Gilbert, 88-92. Guilford, CT: McGraw Hill / Dushkin, 2002.

Phares, E. Jerry, and Nancy Erskine. "The Measurement of Selfism." *Education and Psychological Measurement* 44 (1984): 597-608.

Piorkowski, Geraldine K. *Adult Children of Divorce: Confused Love Seekers.* Westport, CT: Praeger, 2008.

Popenoe, David, and Barbara Defoe Whitehead. "The State of Our Unions: The Social Health of Marriage in America." *National Marriage Project.* New Brunswick, NJ: Rutgers University, 1999.

Quoidbach, Jordi, Elizabeth W. Dunn, K. V. Petrides, and Moira Mikolajczak. "Money Giveth, Money Taketh Away: The

Dual Effect of Wealth on Happiness." *Psychological Science* 21 (2010): 759-763.

Raskin, Robert, and Howard Terry. "A Principal-Components Analysis of the Narcissistic Personality Inventory and Further Evidence of Its Construct Validity." *Journal of Personality and Social Psychology* 54 (1988): 890-902.

Rector, Robert E., Kirk A. Johnson, Lauren R. Noyes, and Shannan Martin. *The Harmful Effects of Early Sexual Activity and Multiple Sexual Partners among Women.* Washington, DC: Heritage Foundation, 2003.

Reid, David, E. Jane Dalton, Kristine Laderoute, Faye K. Doell, and Thao Hguyen. "Therapeutically Induced Changes in Couple Identity: The Role of We-ness and Interpersonal Processing in Relationship Satisfaction." *Genetic, Social, and General Psychology Monographs* 132 (2006): 241-284.

Rempel, John K., and Christopher T. Burris. "Let Me Count the Ways: An Integrative Theory of Love and Hate." *Personal Relationships* 12 (2005): 297-313.

Revenson, Tracey A., Karen Kayser, and Guy Bodenmann. *Couples Coping With Stress.* Washington, DC: American Psychological Association, 2005.

Richardson, Ronald W. *Family Ties That Bind: A Self-Help Guide to Change Through Family of Origin Therapy.* Bellingham, WA: Self-Counsel Press, 2009.

Roberts, Linda. "Fire and Ice in Marital Communication: Hostile and Distancing Behaviors as Predictors of Marital Distress." *Journal of Marriage and Family* 62 (2000): 693-707.

Robinson, Jonathan. *Communication Miracles for Couples: Easy and Effective Tools to Create More Love and Less Conflict.* Newburyport, MA: Conari Press, 2012.

Rotter, Julian B. "Generalized Expectancies for Internal Versus External Control of Reinforcement." *Psychological Monographs* 80 (1966): 1-28.

Scarf, Maggie. *September Song: The Good News about Marriage in Later Years.* NY: Riverhead Books, 2008.

Schaeffer, Brenda. *Is it Love or Is It Addiction?* Center City, MN: Hazelden Press, 2009.

Schwartz, Barry. "Self-Determination: The Tyranny of Freedom." *American Psychologist* 55 (2000): 79-88.

Schwartz, Barry. *The Paradox of Choice: Why More Is Less.* NY: Harper Collins, 2004.

Schwartz, Barry, and Andrew Ward. "Doing Better but Feeling Worse." In *Positive Psychology in Practice,* edited by P. Alex Linley and Stephen Joseph, 86-104. NY: Wiley, 2004.

Schwartz, Barry, Andrew Ward, John Monterosso, Sonja Lyubomirsky, Katherine White, and Darrin R. Lehman. "Maximizing Versus Satisficing: Happiness Is a Matter of Choice." *Journal of Personality and Social Psychology* 83 (2002): 1178-1197.

Scott, Shelby B., Glenda K. Rhoades, Scott M. Stanley, Elizabeth S. Allen, and Howard J. Markman. "Reasons for Divorce and Recollections of Premarital Intervention: Implications for Improving Relationship Education." *Couple and Family Psychology: Research and Practice* 2 (2013): 131-145.

Seider, Benjamin H., Gilad Hirschberger, Kristin L. Nelson, and Robert W. Levenson. "We Can Work It Out." *Psychology and Aging* 24 (2009): 604-613.

Seligman, Martin E. P. *Authentic Happiness.* NY: Free Press, 2002.

Shiota, Michelle N., and Robert W. Levenson. "Birds of a Feather Don't Always Fly Farthest." *Psychology and Aging* 22 (2007): 666-675.

Shoda, Yuichi, Walter Mischel, and Philip K. Peake. "Predicting Adolescent Cognitive Self- Regulatory Competencies from Preschool Delay of Gratification." *Developmental Psychology* 26 (1990): 978-986.

Simpson, Jeffry A., Bruce Campbell, and Ellen Berscheid. "The Association Between Romantic Love and Marriage: Kephart

(1967) Twice Revisited." *Personality and Social Psychology Bulletin* 12 (1986): 363-372.

Smith, Marilyn, Barbara Nunley, and Evelyn Martin. "Intimate Partner Violence and the Meaning of Love." *Issues in Mental Health Nursing* 34 (2013): 395-401.

Sophia, Eglacy, Hermano Tavares, Marina P. Berti, Ana Paula Pereira, Andrea Lorena, Cidalia Mello, Clarice Gorenstein, and Monica Zilberman. "Pathological Love: Impulsivity, Personality, and Romantic Relationship." *NCS Spectrums* 14 (2009): 268-274.

Spilka, Bernard, Ralph W. Hood, Bruce Hunsberger, Richard Gorsuch. *The Psychology of Religion.* NY: Guilford, 2009.

Stafford, Laura, and Daniel J. Canary. "Equity and Interdependence as Predictors of Relational Maintenance Strategies." *Journal of Family Communication* 6 (2006): 227-254.

Stanley, Scott M. *The Power of Commitment.* San Francisco: Jossey-Bass, 2005.

Stanley, Scott M., Sarah W. Whitton, S. L. Sadberry, Mari Clements, and Howard J. Markman. "Sacrifice as a Predictor of Marital Outcomes." *Family Process* 45 (2006): 289-303.

Strepp, Laura Sessions. *Unhooked.* NY: Riverhead Books, 2007.

Sternberg, Robert J. *Love the Way You Want It.* NY: Bantam Books, 1991.

Sternberg, Robert J. "The Triangular Theory of Love." In *Close Relationships,* edited by Harry T. Reis and Caryl E. Rusbult, 213-227. Philadelphia, PA: Taylor and Francis, 2004.

Stosny, Steven. *You Don't Have To Take It Anymore.* NY: Free Press, 2006.

Strong, Greg, and Arthur Aron. "The Effect of Shared Participation in Novel and Challenging Activities on Experienced Relationship Quality." In *Self and Relationships,* edited by Kathleen D. Vohs and Eli J. Finkel, 342-359. NY: Guilford, 2006.

Sussman, Steve. "Love Addiction: Definition, Etiology, and Treatment." *Sexual Addiction and Compulsivity* 17 (2010): 31-45.

Tangney, June P., Roy F. Baumeister, and Angie Luzio Boone. "High Self-Control Predicts Good Adjustment, Less Pathology, Better Grades, and Interpersonal Success." *Journal of Personality* 72 (2004): 271-324.

Teachman, Jay. "Premarital Sex, Premarital Cohabitation, and the Risk of Subsequent Marital Dissolution among Women." *Journal of Marriage and Family* 65 (2003): 444-455.

Thompson, Laura Yamhure, C. R. Snyder, Lesa L. Hoffman, Scott T. Michael, Heather N. Rasmussen, Laura S. Billings, Laura Heinze, Jason E. Neufeld, Hal S. Shorey, Jessica C. Roberts, and Danae E. Roberts. "Dispositional Forgiveness of Self, Others, and Situations." *Journal of Personality* 73 (2005): 313-357.

Tsang, Jo-Ann, Wade C. Rowatt, and Ruth K. Buechsel. "Espressing Gratitude." In *Positive Psychology: Exploring the Best in People,* edited by Shane J. Lopez, 37-53. Westport, CT: Praeger, 2008.

Tsapelas, Irene, Arthur Aron, and Terri Orbuch. "Marital Boredom Now Predicts Less Satisfaction Nine Years Later." *Psychological Science* 20 (2009): 543-545.

Twenge, Jean M. *Generation Me.* NY: Free Press, 2006.

Twenge, Jean M. "Narcissism and Culture." In *The Handbook of Narcissism and Narcissistic Personality Disorder: Theoretical Approaches, Empirical Findings, and Treatments,* edited by W. Keith Campbell and Joshua D. Miller, 202-209. Hoboken, NJ: Wiley, 2011.

Twenge, Jean M., and W. Keith Campbell. *The Narcissistic Epidemic: Living in an Age of Entitlement.* NY: Free Press, 2009.

Twenge, Jean M., and Joshua D. Foster. "Birth Cohort Increases in Narcissism Personality Traits Among American College

Students, 1982-2009." *Social Psychological and Personality Science* 1 (2010): 99-106.

Twenge, Jean M., Sara Konrath, Joshua D. Foster, W. Keith Campbell, and Brad J. Bushman. "Egos Inflating Over Time: A Cross-Temporal Meta-Analysis of the Narcissistic Personality Inventory." *Journal of Personality* 76 (2008): 875-901.

Twenge, Jean M., Liqing Zhang, and Charles Im. "It's Beyond My Control: A Cross-Temporal Meta-Analysis of Increasing Externality in Locus of Control, 1960-2002." *Personality and Social Psychology Review* 8 (2004): 308-319.

Vaillant, George E. *Triumphs of Experience: The Men of the Harvard Grant Study*. Cambridge, MA: Harvard University Press, 2012.

Van Epp, John. *How to Avoid Marrying a Jerk*. NY: McGraw Hill, 2007.

Van Epp, John. *How to Avoid Falling in Love with a Jerk*. NY: McGraw Hill, 2008.

Vohs, Kathleen D., Catrin Finkenauer, and Roy F. Baumeister. "The Sum of Friends' and Lovers' Self-Control Scores Predicts Relationship Quality." *Social Psychological and Personality Science* 2 (2011): 138-145.

Waite, Linda J., and Maggie Gallagher. *The Case for Marriage*. NY: Doubleday, 2000.

Wallerstein, Judith, and Sandra Blakeslee. *The Good Marriage: How and Why Love Lasts*. NY: Houghton Mifflin, 1995.

Walsh, David. *No: Why Kids of All Ages Need to Hear It and Ways Parents Can Say It*. NY: Free Press, 2007.

Wegscheider-Cruse, Sharon. *Another Chance*. Palo Alto, CA: Science and Behavior Books, 1989.

Weigel, Daniel J., and Deborah S. Ballard-Reisch. "Relational Maintenance, Satisfaction, and Commitment in Marriages." *Journal of Family Communication* 8 (2008): 212-229.

Weiner-Davis, Michele. *Divorce Busting: A Step-by-Step Approach to Making Your Marriage Loving Again.* NY: Fireside Books, 1993.

Weiner, Davis, Michele. *The Sex-Starved Marriage.* NY: Simon and Schuster, 2003.

Weiss, Robert, and Jennifer Schneider. *Untangling the Web.* NY: Alyson Books, 2006.

Welch, Kelly J. *Family Life Now.* NY: Allyn and Bacon, 2010.

Whitaker, Carl, and Augustus Napier. *The Family Crucible.* NY: William Morrow, 1988.

White, Richard, John Cleland, and Michel Carael. "Links Between Premarital Sexual Behavior and Extramarital Intercourse: A Multi-Site Analysis." *Aids* 14 (2000): 2323-2331.

Whitehead, Barbara Dafoe., and David Popenoe. "The State of Our Unions: Who Wants to Marry a Soulmate?" *National Marriage Project.* New Brunswick, NJ: Rutgers University, 2001.

Williams, Brian K., Stacey C. Sawyer, and Carl M. Wahlstrom. *Marriages, Families, and Intimate Relationships.* Boston, MA: Allyn and Bacon, 2009.

Wilson, Beth. *He's Just No Good for You.* Guilford, CT: Globe Pequot Press, 2009.

Wood, Julia T. *Interpersonal Communication.* Belmont, CA: Wadsworth, 2012.